The Ascension Companion

Booklocker.com, Inc.
2006

The Ascension Companion

A Book Of Comfort For Challenging Times

Karen Bishop

Also by Karen Bishop

Remembering Your Soul Purpose: A Part Of Ascension

The Ascension Primer
Life In The Higher Realms Series: Book One

TABLE OF CONTENTS

INTRODUCTION

THIS BOOK WAS CREATED with you in mind. At times through the ascension process, we can become confused, and having some validation can be greatly soothing. With so much occurring for us, within and without, it's a miracle if we can see the forest for the trees!

The ascension process is affecting many of us on planet Earth. (For a detailed description of this process and what it involves, why it is occurring, and how we are being affected, you may find these answers in *The Ascension Primer*.) *The Ascension Companion*, then, was designed similar to a card deck, but within a book. Open at random to any page, and you will be guided to a message that is just for you at this particular time in your experience. Or you may choose to intentionally choose a topic that particularly resonates with you.

Each of the 33 topics or messages, contains an explanation of what and why this experience is occurring, usually along with a higher realms picture of what this experience is designed to create within you. In this way, you will know what you are gravitating towards or "morphing" into and why. The messages then, serve as your roadmap to a higher realms reality.

As you open the book to any page, you will be validated that all is in divine and perfect order, as the messages will serve to explain and make clear why this sometimes strange and confusing experience is happening for you. Other messages contain information on ways to connect more fully to the higher realms, in order to support your process. All in all, a higher realms way of living and being emerges through these pages in one way or another.

It is my greatest desire that this book serves to bring you comfort and security during your ascension process, and serves as a reminder that there is order and security at every turn of our evolutionary process. As a loving companion, here to serve and support you, may *The Ascension Companion* be your good friend in times to come.

Wishing you Heaven in your heart, starlight in your soul, and miracles in your life during these miraculous times,

Karen

ACCEPTANCE

...

ENERGY FLOWS MUCH more easily through an open channel. If you have ever had any training in psychic development, the first thing you are taught is how to relax. This opens your channel. If you practice yoga, you may have found that this experience opens you as well. Whenever I do yoga, I end up getting huge downloads of information, as this wonderful act of opening up always serves to connect me.

Acceptance and allowing can greatly help your ascension experience by creating an open channel. Anytime that we resist, we block the flow of energy. Through the ascension process, we are frequently receiving large amounts of much higher vibrating energy. The higher vibrating energies are arriving in quantities and in vibrations that enable us to acclimate and assimilate them...even though at times this may not seem to be the case. We are being stretched as far as we can go, so that this process can continue at a fairly good rate. The reason we experience discomfort either through our physical form or through our emotions, is because these higher energies are hitting areas of denser energies, or blockages. If you have had an injury of some sort, either physically or emotionally, you will know it when these energies arrive....as these areas feel it the most. They are the most out of alignment.

If we intentionally block the process through resistance and fear, it only makes things worse. If we decide that we are not willing to have this ascension process, as it is much too difficult, our resistance serves to block these higher vibrating energies and we can get thrown into a tizzy of confusion, panic, and depression.

By **accepting** that the ascension process is one of a divine nature, and by remembering that we are the ones who instigated it and are choreographing it, it can greatly ease the process. By knowing that all is in divine and perfect order, and that there is absolutely nothing "wrong," we can then relax a bit more and **allow** this process to do what it is designed to do.

As much of the darker and denser energies are up and out, due to the purging that ascension creates, we must know that things are not getting worse, but getting better. Even though it may appear that all has gone haywire in the world, things are actually only getting to a place where they are truly *visible*, so that change can occur through a desire and summoning of the masses. In this way, it can greatly help to **accept** this process and **allow** it to occur.

Acceptance has another role as well. We cannot move forward with any form of creation, until we **accept**, **become**, and **be** where we currently are. By **accepting** where we are and by knowing that we are right where we need to be, we can then free up the energies that carry us and enable us to move forward again.

Acceptance creates a space of letting go and of release. It creates an energetic space similar to the space in between thoughts during meditation. It creates a space of non-attachment to any outcomes or agendas, which is the way of the higher realms. It places us in the moment, and this is precisely when creation occurs. It is the space of neutrality.

If you have chosen this page, you are being encouraged to let go and appreciate where you currently are. If you can believe that there is a reason for your current experience, as it is most likely here to support you in your growth and expansion, you will again move forward with great ease. By knowing and **accepting** that what is occurring for you comes from the divine, with a divine purpose that is truly supporting you, you will be **allowing** much more energy to flow through you and connect you at higher levels.

APATHY

...

"I DON'T KNOW WHAT'S wrong with me these days. I just don't seem to care about much of anything anymore." "I seem to have lost all interest in becoming involved with the things that I used to." "I don't care what happens." If you have had any of these thoughts or feelings lately, know that they are a regular part of the ascension process and have a perfect and distinct purpose.

At times, we may feel as though we are going along, "acting" our way through our daily lives. We are simply not present, as our lives do not have the meaning that they used to. We don't seem to be in alignment with what we had created in the past. And in addition, becoming exhausted through all the trials and tribulations that ascension can bring, can make one very **apathetic**. We are just too darned tired to become involved with or care about much of anything. "Let the chips fall where they may," becomes our general course of action (or *in*-action!). "I no longer have the desire to stay on top of things."

But **apathy** has a gold nugget within it. Being **apathetic** actually places us in a higher vibrating space. It supports our continual process of letting go of attachments. When we no longer care about much of anything, we then become un-entwined with much. We are then left in a space of "no space," and this is the space of the higher realms. We are then much more in the moment. When we do not care about much, we are not filling our thoughts and emotions with things that are not really "real." And we are much more out of the way.

In the higher realms, there are no agendas and plans. With no attachments, with a good connection to Source, with great trust, and a knowingness that everything is always in divine right order, nothing really matters anyway. Being much more connected to Source on a continual basis, keeps us more even keel. There aren't as many ups and downs. And when we realize that things are really no big deal, as we can create fresh and New within any given moment, **apathy**, then, fits right in.

In order to create successfully, we have to have no attachments. It is always precisely when we no longer care about having something, that it arrives. And we do not really want to create from our ego or dis-connect selves anyway. As we progress through the ascension process, then, and become used to not having much of anything go our way, or how we had imagined, we are certainly placed smack in the middle of a higher vibrating space. These experiences force us to let go. Isn't it strange that the areas in our lives that we do not have strong opinions about, seem to always go along just fine?

I had a web designer who decided that she was going to retire from all computer work and web design. The trials and tribulations that her work was bringing were no longer worth it for her. The minute she let go and gave it all up, she immediately began to get huge amounts of business, and the new clients were the kind she has always wanted. It was when she no longer cared about web design, as she was really burned out, that her business really took off. (She still quit anyway!)

When things don't go our way, many times it is because we are not coming from our "connected" self. We may be coming from a desperate or analytical self that is trying to solve a problem is a way that we feel is *possible*... even if we aren't even particularly wild about our own idea. If we were to look back, we would usually find that we were glad this or that had never happened. Being in a state of **apathy**, caused by never seeming to get what we want, among other things, puts us in that space of neutrality where we can create just about anything. When we realize that nothing really matters much, as what we thought mattered was coming from our dis-connect selves, it is then that we are successfully reaching the higher realms. Being happy where we truly are, always brings the next step of creation to our doorstep.

When we have to have things a certain way, we basically place a choke hold on energy. It is when we can be contented by simply **being**, that all our needs are met. Passion is a seeming contradiction to this scenario, as passion is a *very strong* connection, because we know that what we are passionate about is in perfect alignment in every way with our higher selves. So there is a distinct difference in regard to passion. We usually experience **apathy** when we are releasing desires that arise from our dis-connect self. We didn't need them anyway.

If you have chosen this page, you are being encouraged to honor your state of **apathy**, and to realize that **apathy** is a condition of the higher realms. It is an indication that you are vibrating higher and becoming a higher level being. Feeling **apathetic** is simply great training for a higher level way of being. Congratulations, as you are learning the non-attached state of neutrality.

BEING

...

BEING IS A STATE that the ascension process desires to place us in...permanently. When we are in a state of **being**, it affects much. And it most certainly places us in a higher realms reality and way of existing.

Through many of the experiences of ascension, we are encouraged and supported (and many times "forced") into situations that require us to simply **be**. A common ascension experience involves a health crisis, where we are forced to get out of the way and are unable to "do" anything on our own. Another scenario involves the exhaustion that ascension brings, as we are "morphing" and re-wiring into a higher level human. When continually exhausted, we are again, unable to "do." With the continual beating down that we receive through ascension, we can many times become apathetic and begin to not care like we used to. Here again, is another way that we are being encouraged to simply **be**. These are but a few of the ways that the ascension process perfectly grooms us for this state of **being** that is necessary for living in the higher realms.

So why is **being** so important and necessary? **Being** is a state that gets us out of the way. As we are so rapidly losing our disconnect, or ego selves, which are so very used to running the show, a state of **being** is where we are most certainly headed. When we are engrossed in a creative project, allowing Source energy to flow through us so effortlessly, we are in this state of

being. This state is also the place of neutrality, it's the space we come from when we have no agenda, and it's where we go when we are simply enjoying the beauty of nature. This is the state to be in if we want to connect to higher level beings more easily, and even connect to our higher selves (which is the same thing!).

A state of **being** is important to the ascension process because it brings us much more closer to being Source ourselves. It greatly opens the doorway to our connection. And within this connection, we are then able to create from our connected self instead of our dis-connect, or ego self. **Being** also places us in the moment, and within the moment is all there is. It is all that can possibly exist. It is the NOW.

Creating can only come from a state of **being**. We very *un*-intentionally create most of everything according to how we are vibrating. How we are **being**, or vibrating, determines what experiences and realities we will attract to us. Creating the higher realms way, involves letting go and getting out of the way. As we are now embodying much more of the feminine energy, as this is the way of the higher realms, "doing," which is the masculine, is falling by the wayside. In the higher realms, creating involves *intent* (the masculine...without the "doing"), *allowing* or receiving (the feminine), and *being* (Source). The formula for creating would then be to put out an intent, allow for it to arrive, all while being in your joy, passion, and whatever keeps you in a higher vibration.

In this way, "doing," or making things happen yourself through sheer effort, is a thing of the past. Ascension makes us too tired and apathetic anyway! Connecting with Source and becoming a partner, connects us for purposes of creating, as well as allowing us to create from a much higher state with much higher vibrating desires. We can allow Source to do the work while we are simply **being**!

There are many days when I will simply sit with my cat Ahmee and become one with nature and the sunshine. Total silence and pure bliss. We are simply **being**. Animals innately know how to do this. They are in this way, very connected to Source. They know how to be in the moment. If I get caught up in publishing details and the old 3D world, I can only take it for so long, and then I have to get back into a state of **being**.

If you have chosen this page, you are being reminded that you do not have to do it all yourself. If you can, take a day designated just for you and do whatever you want, even if it makes no sense. See what your day brings and where you end up. No planning...just **being**. Or try and become engrossed in a creative project and see how the day flies by. Even simple yoga stretching (not the vigorous kind), can place you in a state of **being**, as you hold a posture for a long time.

Allowing yourself to bask and be present is a way of the higher realms. Enjoy!

BIRTH

...

THROUGH THE ASCENSION process, as we know, we are literally dying while in a 3D body. Just like the death experience in the old 3D world, we are experiencing a vast amount of letting go and releasing much that is not of a higher dimensional way...all in order to arrive in a higher dimension. Only this time we are taking our physical bodies with us.

As we begin arriving on "the other side," we are also basically being re-incarnated again. This re-incarnation experience, without the usual 3D death experience, can create some interesting phenomenon. And it is not sudden, like the 3D death process...it is gradual, which can make things even more confusing.

Before the ascension process really began in earnest, in 2000, we had different roles. Lightworkers came to the planet to begin the "shake-up" process with the energy...to raise the consciousness of the planet and get things rocking and rolling for the ascension process to take hold. This was the primary role and purpose of the "first incarnation."

After critical mass was reached on the planet and it was time for many to "cross over" in January of 2006, a massive **re-birth** occurred, and many were then ready for a very New role. But there were also those who went way ahead, and thus experienced a **re-birth** far before the critical mass.

After the critical mass had a **re-birth** experience, they were then ready for a very New purpose and role. They had basically reached a critical mass within themselves, and were now vibrating at a much higher level. During this time, then, the New roles involved the creation of the New Planet Earth. They had left their old roles and purposes behind. And much of their old selves too!

Birth is a very key component of the ascension process. I remember having a **re-birth** experience several years ago. I was checking in, or basically giving myself a reading, and all I could see was me waving good-bye and crossing over through some big energetic doorway into another world and reality. I have to say, that at the time, this really freaked me out. This was long before we really knew much about ascension. I thought I was probably getting ready to die. And then, sure enough, I had a substantial and intense ascension process all in one big "whoosh!", and thought I was certainly going insane.

But I emerged in a totally New space, and felt incredibly wonderful and much stronger than I had ever been in my other life. I had let go of a lot and greatly changed my vibration. The ascension process creates many **re-births**. There is not just one. I have had several. Many times they arrive around the time of our birthdays. I usually know when one is about to occur, as I feel that I am going somewhere, along with feelings of great loss and sadness...knowing that much will be left behind. And I usually feel a bit panicky as well. I feel that at some level, I am going somewhere that I have never been before...some unknown place. But also knowing that so many will be ascending in the future, can bring great comfort that some of our loved ones will be arriving one day as well.

Through a New **birth**, relationships with our old 3D physical families can be greatly affected. We chose these physical families for very specific reasons in our first incarnation involving the ascension process. When we re-incarnate, we are not attached to them anymore. It is not uncommon to lose contact and to then leave these original physical families. It is part of the process. Maintaining a relationship out of pure love and affection, can keep these relationships afloat...so we do not necessarily have to say good-bye to our biological families. But our soul families will arrive in due time...especially our connections to our teams for creating the New World, and we will feel connected once again, only for different roles and purposes. We will then be having very New families and at a much higher level.

After the first **re-birth**, we usually lose most of our damaged inner child energy. It is replaced by the energy of the original innocence. We are then coming from much more of a Source connection, instead of coming from our ego, or dis-connect selves. It is truly a wonderful space to now be in.

If you have chosen this page, you are going through a **re-birth**. Although you may feel distraught, stressed, confused, and anguished, know that you will feel so incredibly cleansed and divine after your New **birth** is complete. Happy Birthday and get ready to welcome to a very New you! It is truly worth it in the end!

BODY SUPPORT

...

THIS JOURNEY OF ASCENSION is certainly an amazing and one-of-a-kind experience. It affects us at all levels, and our physical vessels, or **bodies**, go through much. Firstly, those who came to greatly assist and begin the ascension process, the lightworkers, agreed to be born into challenging situations in order to transmute the lower vibrating energies. The lightworkers, then, chose to em-**body** these energies. And then, as the ascension process greatly accelerated in the year 2000, this process affected many at physical levels as they were literally mutating, or transforming into a higher vibrating human. This transformation, or transmutation, affects the **body** at cellular levels. And in addition, the body is losing much of its density as well, as it needs to lighten its load in order for a residency in a higher vibrating dimension of the higher realms.

So you can see then, how our **bodies** are really going through the ringer. They greatly assist with the transmutation process. Consciousness cannot expand unless it is in form, and our **bodies** are the form. Exhaustion and severe fatigue are mainstays of ascension. So are various aches and pains in about every spot you could imagine. And strangely enough, as our bodies complete the various stages of alignment through transmutation and/or embodiment, these strange and unfamiliar aches and pains seem to simply vanish on their own.

17

Body support can greatly assist is the process and help to diminish some of these uncomfortable symptoms of evolution. A general rule of thumb in regard to **body support** is that:

*Anything **of the earth** will greatly assist in placing you in alignment with the higher realms and higher vibrating energies.*

The door to the higher realms comes from within the earth and within ourselves, plain and simple. It is not up in the sky or somewhere "out there." The earth is the catalyst and the doorway to the higher realms. Therefore, anything that contains the energy or substance of the earth, will place you in alignment with the higher vibrations and can greatly ease the discomfort that comes from any mis-alignments.

"What exactly does this mean?" you may be wondering.

Here are some specific examples of support that may be of help:

- Water is key. And it is best that it is salt water or water containing magnesium. We are comprised of water, and so is the earth. Drink a lot of it, shower in it often and swim in it whenever possible. It acts like a buffer and helps to tone down and wash away alignment symptoms.
- Make sure you are consuming enough minerals. Minerals come from within the earth. Muscle cramps can occur from the ascension process and electrolytes and trace minerals added to your drinking water can help. Remember, we are the earth.
- A gentle, stretching type of restoration or kundalini yoga greatly assists in placing one in alignment with the higher realms. Holding a posture for a long period of time takes you through all the layers, so to speak, and really lines you up and connects you. This type of yoga is good on a regular basis.

- Eat organic and raw as much as possible. The earth is being restored to its original blueprint through the ascension process, and basically going organic, or back to its pristine state. Eating organic, then, will place you in alignment. In addition, it greatly assists with the purification process. The more purified we are, the easier it is to reside in these higher vibrating energies.
- Exercise often. It keeps the energy flowing. A good daily walk in nature can be enough.
- Spend time in nature as much as possible. Simply lying on the earth can line you up immediately. And any nature above 7,000 feet is even better, as the higher elevations are above the mass consciousness.

If you can get in the habit of really taking time for yourself, this is part of **body support** as well. Simplify your life, be out in nature as much as possible, and make yourself a priority.

If you have chosen this page, you are being reminded to take care of yourself. By practicing regular habits of **body care**, you are automatically in alignment with the higher realms simply through honoring and valuing yourself.

CONFUSION

...

ENTERING THE HIGHER REALMS can really bring about states of **confusion**. Yes, we are beginning a residency in the higher realms, but we haven't completely left the old 3D world yet! Much of what we believed regarding higher ways of being and living were at times inaccurate. This information arrived through a 3D mind, or rather through a dis-connect state of mind. Much of the spiritual information that we were taught, or that we bought into, was therefore coming from a lower vibrating level of consciousness.

As many of us are having some very strange and interesting experiences through the ascension process, we can then become quite **confused** about what is really going on, and what everything was really all about in the first place. Add to this the energy shifts. When we experience an energy shift, it serves to raise our vibration. When this occurs, much of everything within and without is moved around. And during this time of so much "vibration raising," things are adjusting and lining up in regard to a critical mass, so that change can occur. This can cause a **confusing** waiting period. It is no wonder then, that we can become very **confused** at times and not know what in the world is going on!

Confusion can occur when we thought that things would unfold in a certain way. If we were to believe, for instance, that as we raise our consciousness, everything just naturally gets better and better, we would be in for a big surprise. The purging and releasing resulting from the ascension process creates depression and challenging energies, to say the least. And then there are the long periods of waiting, as mentioned above, where we seem to be in a void or in limbo as we are waiting for others to catch up, while we are also "rebooting" or re-aligning for the next step. We may continually expect that the next step will be oh so much better, and then are usually disappointed and let down when it isn't.

Dying while in a 3D body is a very long process. Yes, there are moments of really experiencing great feelings of a higher order, but the process is also *very real*, as it takes us *through* and deeply *into* ourselves. It also seems to stop and start...and this can cause **confusion** as well.

"Have we gotten anywhere at all?" you may wonder at times. Or perhaps you may have had feelings that all this ascension stuff created absolutely nothing New. The truth of the matter is that we have made incredible progress. Taking an entire planet of lower vibrating energy and raising it up is no small matter. Things began at higher levels and then needed to trickle down into the physical. In addition, the lightworkers began their ascension journeys far ahead of everyone else, and therefore have been at it *for a very long time.* This was their service for humanity, and this is one reason why it may seem like things are taking forever. But for others, they have yet to begin.

If you were to look back on what your life was like a year ago, or perhaps even a few months ago, I would imagine you would see that great changes had occurred. You probably are not the same person you used to be and you are also probably in a very different situation in many areas of your life.

Confusion can result when we are seeing a process that does not resemble what we had imagined in our old 3D mind. But our old 3D mind did not know much. For the most part, it was disconnected from Source. And in addition to all of the above, those of us who are here experiencing the ascension process as a service to humanity, are at the helm of the process as well. This means that things can literally change on a dime. At higher soul levels, we get together, have regular meetings, and arrive with a plan. And although there is most certainly a general plan, the logistics and road to get there are subject to "wiggle room." So just when we think we know and understand what will happen next, it doesn't! (Unless, of course, you are very consciously connected to yourself at a soul level...)

If you have chosen this page, you are being encouraged to know that all is *always* in divine and perfect order. Being in the moment can greatly ease any discomforts that **confusion** can bring. If you can get out of the way in regard to analyzing and needing to know, you will connect more greatly to Source in the long-run. The higher we begin vibrating, the more clarity we receive, as we are beginning to "see" things at a much higher level from the other side of the veil. And clarity is not always what we thought it would be! But as we progress further and further along our paths of ascension, we begin to find much more peace, as we truly begin to find the clarity that was always there...we just weren't vibrating high enough to understand it yet.

CONTRAST

...

CONTRAST IS A REALITY of the old 3D world. It was designed to ignite the fire of light with more clarity. By experiencing **contrast**, we are then inspired to summon, or to open up through willingness, in order to create something New and different. **Contrast** shows us what we *do not* want. Knowing what we do not want greatly assists in giving us the clarity we need in order to create what we *do* want.

I remember a time when I was looking for a second residency in Flagstaff, Arizona, as I was about to move to the White Mountains and I wanted to keep a foot back in Flagstaff. I just wanted something part-time that was small and inexpensive. That's all I knew. I hadn't really formulated any big details.

The first thing that arrived was a studio out in the country. This is what I had formulated so far, so this is what arrived. It turned out that there was a shared bathroom in between two studios... and the bathroom was to be shared by a man. The closet was also in the shared bathroom. In addition, there were 12 cats roaming the property and they all had feline leukemia. I had two cats. All this was a sure deal-breaker.

It was then that my friend Donna and I decided to go for a walk around historic Flagstaff to see what was there in regard to small housing. She lived in the area and I thought it would be great to be neighbors. We passed a really cute little townhouse, and I declared, "If this was available, it would be perfect!" Sure enough, it became available within days. Although it was near Donna, as I had wanted, and I had declared it would be perfect, the rent was about the same as the big house I was vacating!

I then decided that I needed a lower rent. Within days, an apartment arrived on the scene that was located on the top floor of an old Victorian house. The rent was perfect. We went to look and it was immaculate. Totally restored, it was huge and a great place for a writer with big picture windows and a *private bath and a huge private closet*. It was also near Donna, BUT... it had no real door...only a big curtain looking over a livingroom, and the kitchen was a shared situation. Hmmmmm...not quite right. And because I had resistance and hesitancy, it rented to someone else within an hour.

In these New and higher frequencies we find ourselves residing in, creation is occurring in record time. Think of something, and it seems to arrive instantly. By experiencing **contrast**, we are then able to experience our creations and truly come to know what they feel like. Any "mis-creations" give us a perfect opportunity to tweak things into the way that we really want them to be.

As we become more and more used to asking for what we want and then getting it, we will then become more and more conscious of what we are really wanting. In the higher realms, creating is very conscious. We do not take what seems to randomly arrive for us. What showed up for is in our old 3D reality was simply a manifestation of what our beliefs were, or how we thought things *could* be. We seemed to go with what was possible in the Old World in relation to the current structures that had been set up, but we need not do that anymore.

Why not consciously create what we truly desire? Although our surrounding reality is surely a manifestation of our beliefs, and it can greatly serve to illuminate what our beliefs are all about, we still have the opportunity to change these beliefs.

Another area where **contrast** is prevalent is within the arrival of an energy shift that carries a specific blueprint. When a New energy arrives, it usually carries with it a specific theme. It first feels wonderful, as this New energy is all about this theme in its highest form. Immediately following the energy surge is the polar opposite of this good and higher feeling energy. We get to then experience the aspects of this "theme" that don't feel as good. Because there is no polarity in the higher realms, these energy surges that contain specific blueprints, or themes, arrive in both higher and lower forms in order to be transmuted and integrated.

Contrast is prevalent here as well. The lower forms of these themes (for instance, unity vs. separation), are set up to inspire us to strive for the higher form. In this way, we reach a balance with the energies. Lower vibrations exist to ignite the fire of creating higher vibrations. In a polarized world, they are what spurs on the light. In the higher realms, this is not the case. The lower vibrations are no longer necessary.

If you have chosen this page, you are being asked to understand the value of **contrast**. If you are experiencing **contrast** in your life, it is there to show you what you *do not* desire, in order to help you to gain clarity for what you *do* desire. And once you let go of any emotions and strong feelings about this situation being shown to you through **contrast**, you will attract the one you *really* want in record time.

DARKNESS

...

I HAVE COME TO KNOW through the ascension process and through experiences in the higher realms, that **darkness** really isn't **darkness** at all. **Darkness** is in fact, greatly tied to the light, as it is the fuel that serves to ignite it. It is the **darkness** that summons the light and allows it to arrive. Whenever I see any **darkness** now, I have to say, I have a great love for it. And the **darkness** loves us too, as it is here in a position of great service in order to get us where we planned on going all along. Without the **darkness**, we would never have accomplished what we have, in regard to raising the vibration of the planet.

A woman in an abusive relationship may be inspired by **darkness** to look within and grow and change. And the person inflicting her abuse knows exactly what he/she is doing at soul levels, as the two planned the whole thing together. It is a great act of love at higher levels. Many times our biological parents created situations that really spurred us on to create and to *be* something different. "I will *never* be like them!" creates exactly the person that you came to be.

Many in the United States have a very unfavorable opinion of President George W. Bush and his administration. But in actuality, he is providing an incredible service and very much involved with the ascension plan at soul levels. At higher levels, he knows exactly what he is doing, and he is doing an incredible and loving job. By providing enough discomfort, contrast, and blatant energies of a darker and denser nature, he is making it near impossible for anyone not to notice or be affected. He is waving a huge red flag that is encouraging the masses to get up off their sofas and out from behind their television sets and ask for something different. He is creating situations that enable many to be willing to let go of what they were holding onto and used to, in order to create something of a much higher order. When things get very uncomfortable, we are then much more willing to let them go.

As I write these words, Al Gore, a prior Vice President of the United States and prior presidential candidate, is releasing his movie and book, *An Inconvenient Truth.* A devoted and passionate environmentalist, this is what he is all about and he has brought this love for the environment to most of his endeavors. He ran for the presidency alongside George W. Bush. He was an environmentalist then and is now. But he lost. Why? Because the planet was not yet ready for his message. George Bush had to win. It was necessary. George Bush has succeeded in getting the masses ready to embrace the higher levels. And so, as I write these words, after 6 years of a Bush administration, Al Gore is being greatly received by many. The hidden agendas and truth regarding the lack of environmental support are now ready to be accepted. The people are finally ready and willing. And they may never have been if it hadn't been for "the **darkness**."

Darkness can really shake us up and encourage us to act in a much higher way. I've been watching things in Africa of late. The atrocities going on there are horrifying and *very dark*. But this continent that is currently experiencing genocide and severe acts of cruelty toward women and young girls, is shining a very bright light. I predict that Africa will be the **darkness** that spurs on the light in a *global* way. The holocaust provided an opportunity for us to say, "This will never happen again." But it has happened again. Things are getting very bad in Africa, in order for the world masses to put a halt to them. We are all one. These things cannot continue on our planet. The summoning of light from situations in Africa will get so bad, until they are noticed by all. In this way, I continually see Africa as a bright and shining light as it is carrying the energy needed to bring in massive amounts of light. In this way, it *is* the light itself. It is the doorway for much light to enter on a global level. Those experiencing these atrocities are incredible beings of light themselves, in order to provide this loving and necessary service...both as victims and perpetrators.

If you have chosen this page, you are being encouraged to see that **darkness** was not what we had interpreted it to be in the 3D world. Everything comes from the light and is here to support us in every way. Things may get *very dark* at times, but when they do, it is only because not enough attention is being placed on the change that needs to occur. Things will get as dark as they need to until illumination occurs. Creating something New and different of a much higher order is what will make us feel good again and place us back into the light. Know that witnessing and experiencing **darkness** does not mean that there is anything "wrong." All, as always, is in divine and perfect order.

DETOXING

...

DETOXING IN REGARD to the human body is a vital part of the ascension process and in a league all its own. For the most part, the ascension process involves a purification, within and without. Anything not matching and vibrating at New and higher levels is basically purged. This occurs in regard to lower vibrating behaviors, perceptions, and various mental, emotional, and spiritual ways. The human body feels the ascension process as well, during times of transmutation and especially at cellular levels as it is the "house" that holds everything. In this way, as the human body loses its' density and serves as a vessel for transmuting, we experience various aches and pains on a regular basis.

But there is also a process involving the human body that is not related to the above. As the earth continues to return to its' organic state, so must our bodies. **Detoxing**, then, involves a cleansing at physical levels. You will know when you are in the process of **detoxing**, because it has its' own special feeling. You may feel like your body is literally rotting. Or you may feel like there is a poison within your system. It just plain hurts. It literally feels as though there are toxins rolling around inside of you, just trying to get out...this is because they are.

One day, I was out in nature in an energetic portal, talking to a Star Being. This particular time, I could almost touch this amazing, huge, and compelling presence. And I felt that we were

33

getting closer to coming to a place where I could see him quite literally and easily in all his glory, just as if he was there in the physical. This day was different somehow in regard to our connection. He was there in more ways than he had ever been. So I asked him, "How can I see and hear you more clearly?" And this was his immediate response: "Purify your body in all ways. By **detoxing**, you can remove the lower vibrating blockages within yourself that hinder our connection."

So it was then that I decided to support this process if **detoxing**, by radically changing my diet and going on periodic cleanses. I really could not believe how naive I had been all this time. I knew I was purifying naturally through the ascension process, but had never even entertained the idea that my eating habits were actually prolonging and hindering the process.

I began to eat mostly raw and organic, go on periodic cleanses, and take daily cleansing herbs. I also began juicing and adding trace minerals to my drinking water, as I had been solely drinking purified water. And I continue to eat this way today. It truly does make a difference.

The more purified we become at all levels, the easier it is to access the higher realms. Lower vibrating *anything*, even food, brings us down into the lower vibrations. By eating better, we literally feel lighter. Any sluggish and heavy feelings seem to greatly lessen. Although we can more easily enter the higher realms by getting out of our own way, if our own way is vibrating higher, we won't need to get out of it so much!

If you have chosen this card, you may very well be **detoxing**. If you are feeling general physical pain all over your body, for no apparent reason, you may be **detoxing**. Supporting this natural part of ascension by purposely **detoxing** your body, can greatly assist you in being in alignment with the higher vibrations. **Detoxing** can help your clarity and concentration, and give you added energy as well. It greatly assists the ascension process in doing what it needs to do.

DISCONNECTED

...

HAVE YOU EVER FELT somehow left out? As if you were perhaps on an island by yourself? Or maybe that things were moving along energetically, and then they suddenly stopped? Have you ever tried to move forward, and been stopped abruptly by some unseen force that simply will not let a thing manifest for you? During this time, have you felt *very unsupported*?

There comes a time with the ascension process when we are basically **disconnected**. The energy that brings in the higher vibrations and this energy that we usually connect to in order to create and move forward, feels simply absent. There are several reasons for this. Basically, *it is* absent. And when these phases occur, they can be quite uncomfortable as they make us feel powerless. And powerlessness is one of the most lower vibrational states we can be in.

We can feel **disconnected** when the energies are re-adjusting. This is a regular pattern with the ascension process. We go through a period of great movement, and then...nothing but stop sign energy. This period of **disconnection** occurs because much is being re-aligned and readied for the next stage of movement. At higher levels and at the lower physical levels as well, things are being moved into place for our arrival. It is as if a bed is being made for us to lie in.

In this regard, we are being prohibited from moving forward for a very good reason. We would not want to move forward into a space or New situation, and then have to move right out of it into a better suited one. Things are being prepared. The energies, so to speak, are elsewhere on a different task that will be highly beneficial to us for the near future.

Several months ago, I needed to register my car in the state of Arizona, as I had moved here a few months prior and had yet to update things. Trying to be a good citizen, I went to the motor vehicle department and "tried" to accomplish this seemingly easy task. Well, evidently, I had brought the wrong documents, and was sent home. A few days later, I tried again, but the lines were unbelievably long, so I decided to wait. While in a neighboring smaller town a week or so later, I thought that I would go to their motor vehicle department, as the wait would most certainly be shorter. As I waited for a little while, an employee soon arrived on the scene and declared that there was a *very unusual* situation at hand, and they were suddenly severely short of staff, so many would need to go home! Well, O.K. Something was certainly up in regard to my car situation. But stubborn me, decided to try one more time. As I was in the *very small* town of St. John's, Arizona, a few days later, I tried again. I was literally the only one in the office that day. "Oh, perfect!" I thought to myself. Well, guess what? I no sooner got my papers filled out than I was told that the computers had just gone down, would be down for who knew how long, and I could not complete my task. In future weeks, my car would suddenly break down and I would end up having to buy a new one...so all was in order, it seemed. (And I ended up buying a brand new car with no source of income and absolutely no credit, as I have no debt!) Although a minor example here of the stop sign energy at work, it can affect us in all areas of our lives, as we seem to literally be held back.

When the **disconnect** phase arrives, it can feel very uncomfortable. No matter what we do or whatever action we take during this time, we seem to get nowhere. Another manifestation during times of **disconnect,** is a lack of support. Supportive finances seem to come to a halt. Nothing seems to arrive for us in any way. It is as if everything has come to one big halt.

Once we know and understand what is going on and why, it can help to ease the frustration of the stand-still energy. If we can trust that this phase is occurring in order to better prepare our place in the future, we can then know that in actuality, we really *are* being supported. As human being we tend to like being in charge of our creations and being the ones to make things happen. With this power seemingly gone, we may feel useless and almost as if our wands have been confiscated or we are being punished for some unknown reason.

But something that knows more than our mental minds know, is very busy creating and lining things up just for us. Perhaps it's about control... a need to be at the helm. But as we connect more and more to Source, we learn to trust that Source can do much of the legwork for us. We simply have to let go and allow, and know that even though nothing seems to be happening for us now, it will again very soon.

If you have chosen this page, know that all is in divine and perfect order. Even though you may feel **disconnected**, things are actually being moved into place to support your next phase. You would not want to move forward into a situation that would soon be changing, along with your own. As you trust that the Universe is on your side, you will soon be in a New and different space that is just perfect for you.

EDUCATION

...

AFTER WE FINISHED much of the higher realms integrating process in May of 2006, we were then poised energetically to really begin creating the New World. For lightworkers, our roles regarding raising the consciousness of the planet had now changed. It was now time to begin implementing the New and bringing it into form. For many who had a role in healing, for example, their practices would rapidly dry up. This was because that role of intentionally raising the frequency of the planet was no longer needed. The planet and her inhabitants had already reached critical mass. This purpose was now over.

The next phase had now begun. It was all about taking our gifts and talents and creating the New...it was about introducing the New ways of being and living on the now very New Planet Earth. In many cases this involved New training and classes for many. **Education** for very New things was now needed.

For the first now completed phase, our concentration was on raising consciousness and vibration. Therefore, many of our dreams, desires and visions that we had when we were very young could not be implemented at that time. It was just not time yet for these visions and dreams to arrive and be a part of the Planet Earth. The earth was not yet ready to embrace and accept them. The earth was not yet a vibrational match. Upon reaching critical mass, that time is finally here. For the most part, we have very New roles now, and some of them need specific training.

If you have had a strong desire since your childhood, to do or create something, now is the time. And if you have been occupied all this time in other arenas, you may not have been able to surround yourself with much in regard to your vision. If you know what you have always wanted to do, and you decide to really go for it, you will most likely be greatly supported in your success. And in many cases, you will need some New and exciting **education** to be able to accomplish what you desire to create.

If you are not sure what it is that you want to become involved with, just start with something. You will know one way or the other if it feels right. If it doesn't, try something else. By simply beginning, you will eventually begin to gravitate and tweak your interests and experiences until they really line up with who you are and what you are here to create. Things will eventually fall into place. I have friends who are taking classes in horticulture, natural cob building, nursing, acting, painting, and so forth.

These New roles that are arriving for us involve our passions and what really lights us up. And these New roles and creations can very well be utilized in a humanitarian way as well. If you have always wanted to be a master gardener or landscape architect, for example, you would be able to utilize this talent in regard to creating an environment that is in alignment with the higher ways of living, *as well as* assisting those who have experienced great loss through a natural disaster. As the old world begins to really fall, it will need to be rebuilt in a way that is in alignment with the higher realms. In this way, our dreams can now be implemented in a variety of arenas.

If you have chosen this page, you are being validated that it is time to take the next step and jump into receiving **education** and training for your New purpose. Your time is finally here.

Trust that the floodgates will open to support you as you begin the next step of creating and assisting with the New Planet Earth. Simply follow your heart and your passion, and that alone will place you in alignment with the higher realms and greatly assist in bringing in the support that you need.

EXHAUSTION

...

"I CAN BARELY WALK across a room." "Just getting through the day is now a big ordeal." "I can no longer do the things I used to. Crashing on the sofa is becoming all too familiar!" "I'm still tired when I get up in the morning." If you have had any of these thoughts, you are not alone.

The ascension process greatly taxes our systems and **exhaustion** is a common and frequently felt by-product. We are really going through the ringer as we begin to vibrate higher and higher while our bodies and all else are restructuring. It is no small feat to change our cellular structure. Not only are we **exhausted** physically, but we are **exhausted** emotionally as well. Thank goodness it was designed so that I would not work during the most intense phases of my ascension process, or I would have been out sick the majority of the time!

As with everything in the Universe, there is divine right order, even with this intense and unmistakable experience of **exhaustion**. Releasing much through the ascension process leaves a pure gold nugget behind. This gold nugget is what remains which vibrates higher...it is what remains when we leave our "in charge" or dis-connect selves behind. Therefore, being **exhausted** creates a state where we simply *cannot* "do" what we used to.

45

In the higher realms, we are in a state of *being*. Through many of the strange stages of ascension, we are being trained or groomed into being the very New Human who resides in the higher realms. This New Human knows how to operate from a state of *being*. No doing or making things happen ourselves...creation and moving energies arrives from our much higher and stronger connection to Source.

Therefore, when we are continually **exhausted**, we can no longer do it all. We are literally forced into a state of surrendering and of *being*. We simply have no choice. This state of **exhaustion** has other by-products as well. In the higher realms, we do not do all the jobs. We are not the bookkeeper, sales rep, mother, father, gardener, *and* housepainter, for instance. In the higher realms, we need only wear one hat. We each have a special gift and a special contribution to make. By being continually **exhausted**, we finally agree to let go of wanting everything the way we want it. We are so very tired, that we cannot wear all the hats. We are then much more receptive to allow others to do what we can no longer do.

The ascension process is designed for us to allow our one gold nugget of purpose to shine through in the higher realms. As each of us makes our unique and special contribution, everything is then accomplished and provided. Trading one gift of purpose, passion, and joy for another, is how we get all of our needs met. What we cannot do or accomplish, someone else will gladly do or accomplish. In this way, we are continually connected through being in our joy.

One day I was writing on my laptop, and thinking that I really needed to weed-eat my yard. I had just bought a weed-eater, done part of it, but was too tired and unmotivated to do the rest. I really never wanted to do it in the first place. It had been on my mind of late, but I was certainly putting it last on the list. Well, suddenly out of the blue, I began hearing the loud noise of a weed-eater outside. As I looked out the window, I saw a team of men in orange suits, weed-eating the side of the road, all through my neighborhood. One particular gentleman, went right into my yard, and weed-eated the whole thing! Task accomplished and I didn't have to lift a finger!

So then, by being **exhausted**, we simply lose our desire to do much. We simply cannot do what we used to. We are too worn out. And again, this state of **exhaustion** places us into a state of allowing and surrendering, therefore connecting us even more. This state of **exhaustion**, then, seems to last for quite awhile. This is so we will really become engrained and proficient in how to simply *be*, while letting others and the Universe take care of things. Getting out of the way through **exhaustion**, is a part of our training for higher realms residency.

If you have chosen this page, you are being encouraged to see what the gift of **exhaustion** brings. As you feel much too tired to do much else, know that you are connecting more strongly now to Source and the higher realms. Know that you are being lovingly watched over by your ascension guide, as you rest and re-wire into the New Human. Your guide will make sure that all your needs will be met, as the non-physical beings so highly revere what we have undertaken, and know that we are greatly helping them as well.

IDENTITY LOSS

...

HAVE YOU EVER found yourself looking in the mirror and wondering who in the world you were looking at? Have you heard yourself talking and thought it was perhaps someone else? Ever felt out of body in regard to who you are? Has you sense of power suddenly departed to who knows where?

If you are having any of these experiences, you have a lot of company...as you are experiencing an on-going part of ascension. The ascension process is designed to connect us to Source. It is designed to throw off and release all the parts of ourselves where we infused our energy since our original conception and separation from Source. As we release more and more of any previous or lower vibrating aspects of ourselves, we then begin to embody more and more of Source energy. We have more "room" within us, so to speak, for this higher vibrating energy to reside.

The old ascension adage is the same...the closer we become to being Source ourselves, the less of our ego, or dis-connect self remains. In order to arrive in the higher realms while still in physical form, we must lose the denser and lower vibrating aspects of ourselves. We developed many traits and characteristics in order to survive in a 3D reality, and now these traits are very rapidly leaving us as they are no longer necessary. To this day, whenever I see the name *Karen Bishop*, I wonder who in the world that is. That name seems to belong to someone whom I am not connected to in any way.

The loss of much of who we thought we were can cause a real **identity crisis**. Who we became in order to get what we wanted, is no longer necessary. In the higher realms we have everything we need. We begin, then, to only be comfortable utilizing energy in one straight and direct shot. Any aspects of ourselves that have developed in regard to agendas, manipulations, or much else that is not "real" and pure are surely leaving at a rapid rate.

This, in turn, relates to our power...or what we thought our power was. It was certainly not *us*, or our dis-connect self. True power is our connection to Source, or rather how much Source we are becoming or *being*. Letting much else go, or having it released for us through the ascension process, can leave one feeling very vulnerable indeed!

"Who am I now?" you may wonder. "What will be left of me?" "I sure don't feel strong or in charge anymore!" These are feelings we all experience through the process of ascension. You are only connecting more strongly and securely to who you *really* are. What will be left intact is the pure gold nugget of the *real* you.

We all arrive here on planet Earth with a specific goal and contribution in mind. The ascension process is designed to spin off and release all the lower and previous aspects of yourself, so that what can remain is the pure form of your original intention. This is why I wrote *Remembering Your Soul Purpose : A Part Of Ascension*. What remains is a very important part of ascension. When we finally arrive so much closer to who we really are...to that beautiful aspect of energy that arrives through our passions and dreams and desires, then we know that we are getting closer and closer to Source.

All lightworkers chose to be born into some conditions of darkness. As said many times before, these conditions were chosen so that lightworkers would be given the opportunity to transmute these energies by embodying them themselves. Consciousness can only evolve through form, and lightworkers were here to raise the consciousness of the planet. In addition, being born into challenging circumstances also served to provide the contrast necessary that would inspire these lightworkers to seek out something higher and better. This contrast was the fire that ignited the light.

The ascension process is greatly assisting in the release of these darker and denser energies. A **loss of identity**, then, is only the loss of these darker and denser aspects that were embodied in order to be transmuted. All is in divine and perfect order.

If you have chosen this page, you are returning to Source and your original blueprint. Although you may have consciously forgotten who you really were, your soul has not. The more you release, the greater your remembrance will be of what your unique and special gifts and talents are. They will come flooding in, in the form of great desires for creativity. Remember, you are only losing what no longer serves you and what is no longer necessary for a life in the higher realms. In the higher realms, it is all about creativity and *being*.

By losing what you thought was your **identity**, you are returning to the original innocence and to who you really are and were meant to be. Welcome back to Source!

ILLUSIONS

...

WHEN WE BEGIN TO raise our vibration through the ascension process, we are then finally able to *really* see what is actually going on. Raising our vibration allows us to see beyond the veil of all the **illusions**. It is as if some cloud cover has been cleared away and now we can see what was really going on all the time. We are no longer, then, viewing things from the mis-perception and filter of our dis-connect selves.

When the **illusions** are finally revealed, it can cause what I call "ascension shock." It is as if we just found out that the two people we thought were our parents for our entire lives, were really our grandparents or perhaps our adoptive parents. When it becomes clear that things were not what we thought they were, it can throw us into a tizzy. But in a very short time, we seem to be able to adjust and move forward, only this time, we are in a very New space of enlightenment.

Breaking the **illusions**, frequently occurs in regard to our personal relationships. We may come to realize, and usually very suddenly, that our most cherished relationships with others were not what we thought they were. In the higher realms, relationships are based upon a mutual love and respect...very simply. If we are having relationships for other reasons, they will blow up in our faces in the higher realms. When the **illusions** are revealed, we may come to see that we were in one relationship because we were lonely, or another because someone was a good listener. Or perhaps one of us was a good supporter, and we needed our needs met and were using another person for this purpose. Or maybe, we even enjoyed feeling important and needed ourselves. The list can be endless, but in the higher realms, we are complete and whole within ourselves and all our needs are met. Therefore, our relationships are based upon love and respect, and a wonderful and special equal purpose of companionship. When we come together as soul teams, another component is added that involves a mutual contribution to the planet, so things get even better!

Illusions can also be revealed in regard to how we thought things worked. At 3D levels, we were only able to explain things and offer stories according to what we could wrap our minds around at a 3D level. As we begin to expand and move into the higher realms, things get moved up a notch or two. We can find through our own personal experiences, that energy and spirituality was not what we had been told it was. Generally speaking, it is much more simple and loving. No lessons to be learned, karma to experience, or any other kind of harsh and consequential "rules." It simply involves learning how energy works and responds. And also knowing that there are higher and lower vibratory levels of energy. The rest is just a game that we made up in order to place meaning and a story on energy movement and manifestations.

Once many of the **illusions** are revealed, we are greatly freed up. No more boxes to fit into or be stuck in, and no more roads that we are forced to travel upon. Without the **illusions**, we can then live the way we were intended to live. The earth was originally created as a playground for experiencing and creating. We can then create whatever we choose when we are free from the **illusions** that were created from a lower level mentality and belief system.

Part of the ascension process involves restoring the earth to this original blueprint; the original blueprint of creating freely from a mindset of no restrictions or lower vibrating beliefs. So then, by suddenly being able to really "see" what was real and what was not, we are following along with the perfect plan of ascension.

If you have chosen this page, you are being asked to realize that **illusions** keep us in a box. By being able to take the plunge of being willing to see that things are not what they seemed, you will be greatly supporting your ascension process. Although it can be difficult to let go of the **illusions**, as they help us to feel secure, there is really more security in the higher realms through our increased connection to Source. Finally being able to "see" can be scary, but as you adjust and go higher, things really get better!

INSOMNIA

...

HAVING TROUBLE SLEEPING? Does it seem like you are up all night, or perhaps you can't really remember if you slept or not? Are you waking up at the same time each night or early in the morning, and unable to get back to sleep? Do you find that even if you are dead tired, or have had little sleep the night before, it doesn't seem to make a difference...you still lie there wide awake for what seems like forever?

Insomnia occurs when we need a break from being in the higher realms, or other dimensions that sleeping creates. We need to be back on the earth plane and it appears that we need to be there or else! Therefore, no matter what we do, we are unable or "not allowed" access to the higher dimensions for awhile...even while sleeping.

One of the most common symptoms of the ascension process, **insomnia,** seems to affect most everyone. And it's a strange kind of **insomnia** at that. It begins by awakening between 2 and 4 a.m. every night for awhile. Then it will subside. It can return again, and eventually, one is awakened around 5 a.m. This can go on for several weeks and then return. Once you wake up, you cannot go back to sleep. Thank goodness the ascension process also has phases of deep sleeping and napping!

Insomnia forces us to remain on the earth plane. We don't get to go anywhere. We cannot go far or deep into other realities for awhile. I personally believe the times that we awaken are related to the dimensions we are in. For example, the hours between 2 and 4 a.m. were universal for most. It was as if we were re-entering the earth plane through the doorway of the 3rd dimension as we gradually began accessing the 4th dimension. It was a year or two before many of us began to awaken at 5 a.m. It was then that we were able to access and be in the 5th dimension.

When we are unable to sleep, we have to then be *here*. Through ascension, we have integrated much and are now vibrating higher. Becoming involved in, and allowing our energy and presence to reside in a New and higher vibrating reality, helps with the integration of a New World and reality. Our presence makes it more real and solid as we are contributing to its very New vibration.

Many times we do a lot of our shifting and releasing while in the dream state at night. Much can happen in regard to our vibrational and spiritual growth when we are asleep. During ascension, *a lot* is occurring for us in this regard. We are greatly changing and expanding in consciousness. Therefore, at times we need a break. We then need to *be* in the New space that we are adjusting to and becoming ourselves.

When I go through periods of **insomnia**, I feel very *here*. There seems to be a lot of energy moving and a lot of energy present. I don't usually feel like I am in much of a restful state...just very present and alert. It can be annoying during these times because no matter what we do, we simply cannot sleep. Craving sleep and rest and becoming frustrated can make things worse. There is absolutely nothing we can do to sidestep this process. Evidently, it is needed. If you are moved to take sleep aids or herbs, you may be able to sleep for very brief periods, but you will still wake up often. It is best to accept this process for what it is, and simply get up and read or something, until it is time to sleep again. This time of no sleep usually lasts for several hours a night. I have some acquaintances who utilized this time to have intimate moments, and now they look forward to the **insomnia**!

If you have chosen this page, know that **insomnia** is a necessary part of the ascension process. No one is punishing us by making us miserable from being sleep deprived. Actually, we are being supported and protected as we go through the process and receive and experience what our bodies need. So pick up a good book or watch an old movie for awhile, until it is time to go back to bed...and enjoy this time as much as you can.

INTEGRATING

...

WHEN HIGHER ENERGY arrives on the planet, it must be **integrated**. Being that these higher energies are New (actually, they are old, and we are just returning to them), they carry within them a theme or blueprint for higher ways of being and living. In order for anything to exist, and especially for anything to be created, we first have to *be* it.

This is why **integrating** the New and higher ways of being is so important. We must totally embody them and *be* them, before they can exist on the planet. It is not enough to know a higher consciousness intellectually. We have to walk our talk. This is all about energy and vibration, not about *knowing*. And after we are done **integrating**, we no longer need to talk about it. We are then *being* it. Continuing to talk about the higher ways of being simply means we are not yet being them.

As the higher vibrating energies arrive, they serve to push out (or purge), any lower vibrating energies within and without. Higher and lower vibrating energies cannot exist in the same space. In this way, there is more "room" within for housing these higher vibrations. After they arrive, the process then begins of **integrating** them.

Integrating manifests in several different ways. If you have ever felt yourself becoming frustrated or *angry* with something that never bothered you in the past, you have most likely **integrated**

a higher version of that situation, and can then no longer tolerate the old scenario. If you find yourself seeing something in a totally New way, from a very different perspective, you have most likely successfully **integrated** a higher way of knowledge and understanding. And in an opposing direction, if you find yourself at peace with a situation that usually bothers you, you have probably **integrated** a higher way of being in some area. Intolerance for a lower consciousness usually means that you have **integrated** much as well.

Integrating also involves our physical selves. Various aches and pains all over your body, feeling like you have been run over by a truck, or perhaps feeling as though you have a bad case of the flu, can mean that you are **integrating** at a cellular level. Your body is acclimating much, and much is changing for you at many levels. Your old cellular structure is being replaced by a New and higher vibrating one.

Another common symptom of **integrating** and aligning is a need to eat often with feelings of low blood sugar. Your body is going through an intense "morphing" and transmutation, and uses up a lot of fuel for this process.

When these New and higher vibrating energies arrive, we have to align with them. They are the New air that we breathe, and we have to be able to "breathe," then, by matching their vibrations. Aligning is what causes the purging. And we have to **integrate** in order to align. Through the ascension process, we continue to align in an on-going way. Believe it or not, we have a long way to go and we are only just beginning! But the further we go, the easier it gets.

Aligning is what it is all about. In order to connect more fully to Source, we need to be in direct alignment. Energy vortexes, for instance, are very much in alignment with higher dimensions and higher vibrations. This is why when you visit a geographical area that has a lot of portals or vortexes, there exist opportunities to access the higher dimensions, as well as having a much greater access to higher dimensional beings. These areas are much more in alignment.

As I write these words, I am in the process of learning cob house building, which will involve building homes from elements of the earth. In this way, these homes will be in alignment with and match the vibration of the earth. In addition, these homes will be placed in alignment with certain celestial bodies and certain planetary alignments which will then support them being in alignment at many levels. Totally sustainable, this will put them in harmony and alignment with the sun, Earth, and moon as well. The higher realms exist within the earth, so this, then, will be a higher form of living and being. It is all about **integrating** in order to be in alignment.

Integrating places us much more in alignment with the higher vibrations. If you have chosen this page, you are in the process of **integrating**. Although you may feel weak and possibly tired, know that you are experiencing a very important part of the ascension process. As you **integrate** the higher ways of being and living, you will come to be much more comfortable living in and creating the New World. Matching this New and higher vibrating Earth will greatly lighten your load and make your life flow much easier as well...and it will absolutely help to ease any discomfort that ascension can bring.

INTOLERANCE

...

SEVERAL YEARS AGO, I had an interesting experience that derived from the arrival of an energy shift. When the higher vibrating energies arrive on the planet, they bring with them opportunities for us to release and align in order to match the higher ways of being that arrive through the shifts. In this way, they serve to assist in raising our own vibrations.

This particular shift arrived in full force and really knocked me off my rocker. It was the beginning of ascension, and not many, if any, knew what was occurring. Also during these early days, there were only a few who were feeling and experiencing the strange symptoms that ascension can bring.

One of the things that began to occur for me was an enormous **intolerance** for anything of a lower vibrating frequency. I had a very difficult time being in the company of anyone who was behaving or emitting energy of a lower consciousness. And any kind of "darkness" made me nearly physically ill.

Immediately, I assumed that I was not being very "spiritual," and began to do inner work on this issue of judgment and **intolerance**. After all, weren't highly spiritual people supposed to be tolerant, loving, and understanding of everything? Weren't these lower vibrational people and ways only manifestations of myself that I was not owning? Wasn't this about integrating and loving the lower aspects of myself?

All of these explanations proved to be totally false. As I grew through my personal ascension process, I began to be able to slowly and surely see beyond the veil of the lower vibrating human. Eventually, it became very clear that **intolerance** was simply a part of the ascension process, and one of many parts that were not how we expected them to be.

As we vibrate higher, we no longer match any lower vibrating manifestations. These denser vibrations, in no matter what form they manifest, feel downright awful to be around. But there is a method and perfectly designed plan to this strange and surprising occurrence.

All dimensions vibrate differently. The higher the dimension, the higher the vibration. This results in a vibrational hierarchy with a perfect order to its existence. As we begin "morphing," so to speak, in order to arrive in the higher realms, we must raise our vibration. Different vibrations cannot exist in the same space. If we are vibrating higher than another vibration, we cannot stay around the lower vibration for long.

This scenario and law of vibrational (or dimensional) hierarchy is evident when we communicate with any non-physical beings. They can come to us for short periods of time. We can communicate with them when we are raising our vibration in some way. One cannot go any higher than they are vibrating, but one can go lower for short periods of time.

This state and experience of **intolerance** is also encouraging us to create something very New and different. Something of a much higher order. This state of **intolerance** will not allow us to remain in the lower vibrating realities. We must, then, begin to create a New World and New reality of our making. As this state of **intolerance** is occurring for more and more individuals every day, it can only serve as a great and perfect plan for igniting the creation of the New.

If you have chosen this page, know that you are well on your way to the higher realms. An **intolerance** for the lower vibrating ways of being is simply an indication that you are vibrating higher. You are being encouraged to leave the old ways and all of the old anything that makes you very uncomfortable, far behind. You are being encouraged to create something of a New and much higher order. You are readying to let go and begin your New residency in the higher realms.

LETHARGY

...

LETHARGY IS A VERY common stage of the ascension process. At times we can feel downright blahhh and not want to do much of anything. Being listless and dragging around with no energy simply means that there is a lot going on within us. We usually feel **lethargic** when we are integrating higher energies. And we can feel **lethargic** when we are getting ready to access the higher dimensions. Both are the same. Barely being able to keep our eyes open, yawning continually, feeling like a dead battery, or feeling like one is walking through quicksand, are very common manifestations of this stage.

When we are "in between" dimensions, we are neither here nor there. This can manifest as feelings of being "not quite here." During these times it can be hard to concentrate, accomplish anything, or even carry on a conversation. We may think that our lives will most certainly fall apart with no one seemingly at the helm, but they do not. I have found through years of ascension, that there is a higher part of us that seems to regulate everything and make sure that all is in order. I have never had a disaster occur at times when I was not functioning at a top notch level...which is a lot of the time!

Lethargy is a different experience and phase of ascension than exhaustion. Exhaustion can go on for quite awhile. Exhaustion is a symptom of a re-wiring occurring at cellular levels. This can take quite a toll on the physical body and utilizes much of our "fuel." **Lethargy**, on the other hand, is more about being in between dimensions as we are readying to arrive more fully in a higher vibrating one. It has a much shorter run time.

The 11th of every month is a pivotal time for **lethargy** to occur, and especially during the time of November 11th, or 11/11. The 11 marks the opportunity for accessing a higher dimension. The higher realms become more available through the pillars of an 11 doorway.

As mentioned before, during these **lethargic** times we usually do not feel as though we are all here. This is because we are not. Part of us is on "the other side," and the rest of us is "here." When a person experiences death through a 3D experience, many times they will go in and out. They will be "out of it" for awhile, and then be back. Eventually, they will lose consciousness and not come back again. During the **lethargic** phase, you may be finding yourself wanting to sleep a lot and take naps when you never have before. Sometimes I wonder if we are going to sleep our way to Heaven! Or at times, cry our way to Heaven!

If you have chosen this page, know that feeling **lethargic** has its purpose and is simply part of the process. You are not lazy, your life will not fall apart, and it's OK to support yourself by lying around for awhile. When you come out of it, you will be much more alive and much more connected to the higher realms, with clear vision and vitality.

LETTING GO

...

LETTING GO, OR "UN-DOING" is probably the most substantial and prevalent theme of the ascension process. As we are literally dying while still in a 3D body, just like the 3D death process, we can't take anything with us. But instead of the instantaneous and massive release in one big "whoosh!" that the 3D death process creates, the ascension process creates a much more gradual releasing and letting go experience. We are most assuredly going to the higher realms, but in a gradual way and while still inhabiting our human form.

In order to arrive in a higher dimension, we have to drop some of our load. We have to lose much of our density. A blob of dense matter cannot be thrust through the fine screen of the doorway to the higher realms. Losing density, or lower vibrating energy, can occur in many ways (as many of the pages of this book will attest), but **letting go** voluntarily can greatly ease the process.

If you have experienced much loss of late, you are very likely in the throes of the process. When we begin to vibrate higher, anything that does not match our current vibration will leave our lives. Energy navigates in a very organized and structured manner. Like energy always attaches to and attracts other like energy. This is a simple law of the Universe. In this way, the ascension process creates losses of jobs, friends, animal companions, homes, personal belongings, and very rapidly, that unsettling loss of identity. And there are times, as well, when we have just finished creating something New and we have to let go of it! It no longer matches our New and higher vibration and purpose.

Letting go is similar to surrendering. The more we let go of, in regard to our internal as well as our external realities and old ways of being and living, the easier and quicker we will arrive in the higher realms. When we continue to hold on to the lower and denser energies, we only create more discomfort for ourselves.

By **letting go**, we then allow the New to arrive. **Letting go** releases us from the Old World and the Old Us. It frees us up to then experience something different that we could not have connected to while we were attached to something else. **Letting go** of a lot, all at the same time, can create a sling shot affect and literally place us in a very New reality that we could not have arrived in before.

By experiencing discomfort created by lower vibrating energies, we are then motivated to let them go. Again, the longer we continue to hold on, then, the more discomfort we will feel until we finally surrender and realize that it is time to move on.

Letting go also involves an "un-doing" process. While residing in a 3D reality, we developed many defense mechanisms in order to survive in this strange and at times challenging world. As we begin to evolve and vibrate higher, enabling us to embody much more of Source energy, we find that we can no longer come from our human ego minds. We must, therefore, let go of all the illusions and mistaken perceptions that we had been navigating from. When we begin to get more and more "connected," we are then able to see what everything is really about. This is why, many times, I feel that the New Age community has the most to let go of or to "undo." They seem to embody the most in the way of misperceptions than the mainstream community does. There are many manufactured New Age beliefs that do not fit in with the higher realms.

We are also **letting go** of all the places where we infused our energy, or incarnated, since the beginning of our original creation. This can manifest as having wild and vivid dreams at night that do not make much sense. And for some, **letting go** of all these past incarnations can even occur in a waking state.

Letting go, or surrendering, can create the most peaceful states that exist. Getting our mental, rational, and ego minds out of the way always enables us to connect to Source very quickly. And Source usually has bigger and better ideas for us than we do anyway! In the higher realms we live in the moment. We know that everything that exists, exists *now*. Higher realms living, again, involves knowing that we always have everything that we need. We will come to know that if we let go of something, we can easily and quickly create something very New at any given moment.

Holding on creates attachments. The ascension process is designed to support us in **letting go** of all attachments. When we are sometimes *forced* to let go, we are then really *experiencing* what it is like to be seemingly hanging out there with no support or security. In time, through the ascension process, you will come to know that Source is all there is. Anything else can be let go of with ease, as creating the New in any given moment becomes a New way of being. Tapping into a different pocket of energy...one that is vibrating much higher...will give you a place to anchor into for awhile.

For example, sustainable living is becoming very popular of late. This is because enough of us are at this level of vibration which involves connecting completely with the earth and living in harmony with her. To live in this way, one would let go of electricity, artificial heat sources, city water and trash, and much else. And having one's own organic garden would enable one to let go of going to the store, for instance. So then, if someone was forced to suddenly let go of what they interpreted as their means of security and survival, they might becoming a little unhinged. But by connecting to a higher way of living and being, they could tap into a New and different reality and be just fine...actually, they would be much better!

Letting go involves stair stepping into New and higher ways, until eventually we have **let go** of nearly everything except Source itself. This is the gradual process of ascension. No one big "whoosh!" Otherwise, we would be dead!

If you have chosen this page, you are being guided and supported in *letting go* of what is no longer serving you. You are being asked to trust that something New and better is on its way for you. Something that fits you much better and will be so much more in alignment with who you are now, is surely on its way. Higher and lower energies cannot exist in the same space. Get ready for something New and better!

LOSS

...

LOSS, LOSS, AND more **loss**. The ascension process is designed to create considerable amounts of **loss**. I suppose that we get used to it after awhile, but in the beginning it can really shake us up. One would think that it would become damaging to the human spirit, but there is a specific reason and purpose for all this **loss**, and things eventually do get better.

If you have ever found yourself crying for no apparent reason, it is usually because you are feeling great **loss**, even though nothing is apparent in your outside reality. Feeling great sadness is also a manifestation of a knowingness at higher levels that much is leaving. Weeping and sadness usually occur when we are losing darker and denser aspects of ourselves. After all, we have lived with these traits for a very long while, and even though it isn't in our best interest to keep them, it is still sad to feel them depart. Sadness usually occurs when much is about to depart at a global level, in regard to the mass consciousness. When we are feeling this overwhelming sadness, most everyone else is as well. We are all in this together.

It can, at times, be confusing to be feeling so much sadness, weepiness, and heightened emotion for no apparent reason, but energetically, there is much going on. These symptoms are simply proof of the pudding.

In addition to much departing in regard to who we are, or old ways and old energy, and many other lower vibrating non-physical creations, we are also experiencing **loss** at physical levels. Friends, relationships, family members, jobs, careers, homes, animal companions, and much of all else in the physical are leaving our spaces at a rapid and regular pace. At one point in my process, I went through a re-birth and lost virtually all of my friends and a cat in one week!

We can experience **loss** in a variety of ways. People in our lives can leave through the 3D death process. These individuals have decided at soul levels that they do not wish to experience the ascension process while in a physical body here on Earth. There are various openings or opportunities that arrive at specific energetic times, and it is during these times that we usually see many individuals departing all at the same time. Of course, people can leave at any time, but these energetic opportunities usually take many people with them. Generally speaking, when souls feel complete with something, they will depart. So then, some stay until a pivotal point is reached energetically on the planet, and others leave when it is right for them and those around them.

Losing those close to us can occur in other ways as well. We generally **lose** people through ascension for two reasons: 1) We begin vibrating differently and this causes a mismatch in energies. Lower and higher vibrating energies cannot exist in the same space for very long, and 2) As the vibration of the planet increases on a regular basis, it then causes New and different scenarios and personal purposes to arise. New roles are then activated for us. In this way, some of us may part in order to fulfill pre-designated roles that we agreed to fill at specific times in our evolutionary process. It can be sad to say good-bye to a good friend because they have a role that is not quite related to yours. But know that we will eventually meet up again in the end.

We can also experience separation or New and unusual feelings regarding our physical families of origin. As we are re-born or reincarnated again through ascension, the purpose of our original family members is no longer needed. This usually creates a different type of relationship or a relationship that ends.

Losing a job results from a disconnect from the Old World reality. We can no longer be involved in these old ways and it is also difficult to work when going through ascension. Our attention needs to be somewhere else as we are beginning to connect more strongly to Source. Most other things that leave us, do so because we are no longer a vibrational match. In order to arrive in the higher realms, we have to be vibrating at the level of the higher realms. As we begin vibrating higher, then, these lower vibrating energies can no longer be where we are or go where we are going.

If you have chosen this page, you are being asked to come to terms with **loss**. As many things leave our lives, better and more suitable things begin to arrive for us. As the New most certainly begins to arrive, it is much more in alignment with who we now are and fits us so much better! Know that you are also becoming lighter and lighter and learning that an attachment to Source is your only real and necessary attachment.

NATURE

···

AS EVERYTHING WHICH resides upon the earth is raising its' vibration and ascending along with the earth, this includes the elements of **nature**. **Nature** can greatly assist us in aligning with the higher realms and in making ascension more comfortable.

The animals and **nature** are already tuned into a higher way of being, for the most part. Whenever you see a horse or animal being still for long periods of time, they are unusually in another dimension. Animals and nature live in the moment as well. They do not pre-plan things and are also very comfortable and used to the death process. They seem to realize that life goes on in one form or another and this is simply a natural process of energy.

Nature knows what is up. If conditions change in regard to supportive habitats, **nature** will either change along with the conditions, or depart, with no resentment. It knows it can re-create itself again and again. And **nature** has higher purposes as well. The pine trees in the forest, for example, are very soothing and literally act as sponges that absorb any extreme or out of balance energy. Every time I spend time at the higher elevations where there are big Ponderosa Pines, I am *always* calmed and soothed.

When I used to give soul readings, I found that there were many individuals here on Earth who were human representatives of the **nature** kingdom. They literally embodied the particular traits of the aspect of nature that they were representing. They were here to show the human community that we are all one. The photographer who took one of my author photos had a pivotal role in regard to **nature**. We had decided to take pictures outside at the higher elevations. As soon as we arrived, the nature kingdom began chattering. They were ecstatic! "He's here! He's here!" they exclaimed. This man was very connected to **nature** as he had been instrumental in setting up the **nature** kingdom on earth eons ago. One would have thought that the **nature** kingdom that day, was witnessing the arrival of their god! This connection and representation of **nature** came through this wonderful man through his photographs. I have never before seen such photographs of **nature**. Photographers are able to access multiple dimensions through their lenses...this is what photography is all about. I have to say, nature was depicted that day in photographs in an amazing way...I only wish I had looked as good. I really felt like an outsider!

Just like connecting with the earth, spending as much time out in **nature** will greatly support your ascension process. **Nature** is tuned in. It is in alignment. It naturally abides by and understands the higher ways of being. It knows how to let go, adjust, bend, be present, and simply *be* who and what it is. And as we are all one, consuming nature products (what *grows*), will also assist in keeping one in alignment with the higher vibrations. Organic basically means returning to a pristine condition. This is what the earth is doing, so consuming anything organic that comes from the earth can help to place us in alignment. I have had several experiences with **nature** when it has served as a great healer. Not only through herbs and flower remedies, for instance, but by lying on the earth and feeling all the nature spirits surrounding me and performing their blissful magic of healing and assisting with alignment. It almost feels like getting Reiki! It is truly glorious.

If you have chosen this page, you are being encouraged to spend as much time as you can in **nature**. If this is not a possibility for you, you can place plants and things that grow, in your home or inside environment. Spending time in **nature** will serve to connect you, calm you, bring you great peace and a sense of remembering in regard to what everything is all about. **Nature** is one of the quickest and easiest ways to connect to the higher realms and bring you into alignment.

PASSION

...

"WHERE HAS MY **PASSION** gone?" you may have wondered at times. "Will it ever return?" "I just don't feel like doing anything," may have been a persistent thought for far too long. Or perhaps, "I don't know what my purpose is, what I am doing here, or even what excites me anymore!"

Passion is one sure thing that returns when much of everything else seems to be leaving our lives. Although it most assuredly leaves for awhile, it always comes back. And when it does, it comes back in a dramatic, intense, and more purified way. Like two ships passing in the night, when the energy surges arrive, out goes the darkness and in comes the creativity.

I can remember a time when I was feeling all the unpleasant feelings that come when we are in darkness...because when it is up and ready to depart, we are really *in* it. But at the same time that the darkness was leaving, intense and compelling amounts of creativity were arriving. What a strange combination of feelings and experiences! But thank goodness for this creativity which arrived through the vehicle of the "pushing" energy surge. It made everything much more bearable. When the higher vibrating energies arrive, they always bring with them higher ways of being and connecting. And creativity through **passion** is a mainstay of the higher ways.

If **passion** were to be defined in energetic terms, it would be all about *non-resistance* in regard to our physical vehicle, which is the conduit for energy to move through. When we are **passionate** about something, we are ready to go for it with absolutely no hesitation. This state of non-resistance, with absolutely no hesitation, creates a very open vessel for energy. **Passion** can occur when we first meet that certain someone. In the beginning, we may think that they are oh so perfect, and therefore, a state of **passion** for them is created. If they have no resistance back at us, then there is *really* **passion**! Planning a creative project can also create **passion**. In order to create this energetic state, we usually plan everything in our minds exactly the way we want them to be. In this way, there is no hesitancy or resistance, and energy therefore pours through in full force.

When we get very **passionate** or excited about something, it is because we feel it deeply at every level and we just *know* it is right. **Passion** exists because we know that something is in alignment with what we are about. When something matches our vibration and our purpose, it then creates a state of **passion**, or uninterrupted energy flow.

Although there exist times during the ascension process when our **passion** is completely gone and we can really feel as though it may never return, it does. Through ascension, we purge and release much of any darker or denser energies within us. These include fear, insecurity, lack of confidence, and a powerlessness to be able to get what we want. After these states begin to leave us, what is then left is a much more defined sense of who we are and why we are here...and what we are here to create! It is then that our **passion** returns.

The higher vibrating energies bring with them great amounts of creative energy. So this part is intact. But what takes awhile is the ascension process itself in regard to releasing the dis-connect parts of ourselves. We cannot be creating from these aspects. We need to be creating from a strong connection to Source. When we feel passion-less, we are simply rebooting and readying for the next phase. All things are coming into a better and higher alignment for the "creating" times to come.

After so much releasing within, we eventually arrive at a place where we are very ready to create through this uninterrupted energy of **passion**. This powerful energy needs an outlet and creativity is then very necessary to our lives. When our **passion** comes in again, it is time to create what you have always been about and what you came to create.

For a long while, my passion was gone, as I was really going through my process. Always a very passionate and exuberant person, I though that I must be getting old or was simply withering away. I didn't know what it was like not to be passionate and so I felt like only half of a person. But passion returns...and especially beginning in June of 2006 for our very New roles. I have never been involved in and more excited about so many different things! From art to humanitarian projects, to much of anything else, I can barely keep up with myself. And with everything falling at our doorsteps in the higher realms, it can be hard to choose!

If you have chosen this page, you are being asked to define your **passion** and begin creating. The energies are most certainly building for you, as you are readying to bring forth something very dear to your heart. When your **passion** returns, it indicates that "all your ducks are in a row," and you have successfully completed the first phase of ascension. Have fun and good luck!

PURIFICATION

...

PURIFICATION IS A NECESSARY and vital part of the ascension process. Because we cannot enter the higher realms, or higher ways of being if we are carrying "suitcases," or denser energy with us, we must then purge or release these lower vibrating energies.

Many of the ascension symptoms exist because we are **purifying** (*The Ascension Primer* book lists 40 of the most common.) **Purifying** through purging, therefore, creates an almost continual state of release within us. Purging involves release through the emotions, as well as through the body. Some common symptoms of purging are:

- Weeping and sobbing for no apparent reason. We release through our emotions and through our tears.
- Diarrhea and skin rashes or skin eruptions. We are releasing lower energies through our natural body functions.
- Nausea and vomiting.
- Anger and frustration. We can become angry when the lower vibrating energies rise within us, ready for release. It's time for a change.
- Changing a residence, career, or leaving a personal relationship. This occurs when we have reached a higher level of being and no longer desire these old energies we had created in our past. We must then release them.

- Wild, crazy, and sometimes violent dreams. Purging through the subconscious is a very common way to process and let go.
- Taking many of your belongings to the Goodwill or some other charity; redecorating, etc. As we begin to change and grow, we are no longer the same person we used to be. Our old belongings, furniture, and such, can feel like they belong to someone else.
- A loss of interest in many of your old activities and ways of living. Same as above, as you are no longer the same person and are ready to let them go.

These are only but a few of the many ways that **purification** through purging can manifest in our lives. It can be very common to have diarrhea for weeks, or suddenly develop a rare case of acne. Just remember to drink lots of water and know that you are being purified in a very natural way. Your soul always knows what it is doing!

Purification and "cleansing" also occur in regard to geographical areas. The New Planet Earth will arise with some geographical areas carrying higher energies than other areas. Although the entire planet is rising in vibration, some geographical areas will become "hubs," or higher vibrating areas with specific purposes or themes.

If these areas are not yet matching the higher vibrations that are arriving, they will experience a cleansing or purification through fire, water, earthquakes, and the like. They will then be ready to be rebuilt in a much higher vibrating way. If they are not rebuilt in a higher way, they will experience more cleansing.
When energy surges and shifts arrive on the planet, they serve to begin this process of purging, cleansing, and releasing. These energies are felt by every living thing on the planet. Therefore, they can manifest not only as purging within each individual, but also in the form of natural disasters. At times, we can feel as

though we have indeed experienced a natural disaster, even though we have not. We are simply feeling these newly arriving energies within us. I call them "internal tsunamis" or "internal earthquakes." They really serve to get things moving. And they can really wear us out, as they are a continual part of the process!

If you have chosen this card, know that all is in order, even though you may feel rattled and even a bit traumatized. **Purification** through purging is a natural and sometimes unpleasant aspect of the ascension process. Things are just moving to the surface to be released. And when this particular phase is complete, you will feel oh so much better... and much lighter!

REMEMBERING

...

WE ARE BORN WITH total memory loss. Of course this is not new information, and most of the time we wish that we weren't. It seems that we can spend the majority of our lives searching and seeking to **remember** what we feel deep inside that is so important...if we could only **remember** what it was!

Feeling like an Alzheimer's patient much of the time, doesn't exactly place us in a space of power in regard to what we came to do here on Earth. It is as if we are reaching into a fog, trying to grasp something that is just out of our reach. And when a message from a channeler comes into our space, we may be inclined to think, "Oh! Some higher information that is from the place that I can't **remember!**" But channeling is only derived from how high the channeler is vibrating, what they are all about, and what their filters are. This is why...**remembering** comes from *within* each and every one of us.

One of the greatest by-products of vibrating higher and higher, is that we begin to **remember**. It is as if a door has opened and we now have access to a New reality and level of knowledge and awareness. But most importantly, we begin to really **remember** *who we are*. We are so much more than we ever thought we were. Most of us have been around for eons of time and are literally ancient. And if we are experiencing the ascension process, it basically means that we are done. We have been around for so long, that we are now complete and ready to move on to a different experience.

Remembering who we are can bring us so much peace and comfort. We are, in essence, reconnecting and reuniting with our true selves. And one thing that **remembering** also does, is to bring us back into our power. This is a very New power. This power comes from a much stronger connection to Source and to our souls (or higher selves). We now know who we really are, and it was not our wounded inner child or any of the other aspects we had evolved into due to challenging experiences of powerlessness.

Remembering who we are and what most of everything is about, puts us back into the driver's seat. We can now create from our connected and higher selves, instead of our ego or dis-connect selves. When we **remember** and know what is really going on, we can then use our will in a more appropriate way. If you have found that you are no longer interested in reading New Age or spiritual material, it is because you no longer need it. You are now more connected on your own.

Remembering also serves to support our ascension process, as it allows us to realize that we were the ones who planned and created this experience in the first place. We then do not have to feel so much like victims. It can remind us of how strong and powerful we really are.

As more and more of the lower vibrating aspects of ourselves fall away, more and more of who we really are at the highest levels begins to emerge and be revealed. Whatever was blocking our connection, is leaving at a rapid rate and enabling us to connect more fully and to **remember**. **Remembering** can bring tears to our eyes. Reconnecting to our Source and to our beginning can feel near overwhelming, and bring emotions of great gratitude as well. It can make us feel oh so much more complete. Reuniting with what feels like the lost or forgotten parts of ourselves makes us whole again, in all ways.

If you have chosen this card, you are well on your way to **remembering**. As the doors to the higher realms begin to open, you will begin to **remember** your place and purpose in all of the cosmos and feel connected like never before.

RESPONSIBILITY

...

RESPONSIBILITY IS GREATLY tied into ascension, as it relates to the old ways of thinking that we have to do everything ourselves. Through the ascension process, we begin to let go of much of our responsibilities. We cannot do it all and we are certainly not responsible for everything...even though many times we seemed to think we were.

The "first wave" of lightworkers, generally speaking, were of baby boomer age. In this way, those who had children were then grown by the time the ascension process began for them, and they were then freed up to experience this unusual and transformative process of ascension. "No attachments" is a good way to describe what ascension strives to create, and in the old world, attachments came with **responsibilities**.

Responsibility comes two-fold in relation to ascension. By *not* connecting or being more in alignment with Source, we then believe that *we* are responsible for most things and especially for making anything happen. Secondly, as we begin to experience exhaustion and letting go through the process of ascension, we are then much more attached to Source, as our lives become much more simplified and pure. So then, through ascension and our arrival into a higher way of being, we come to know that 1) attachments pull us down into a false sense of **responsibility**, and 2) we need only wear our "one hat," or contribute our one pure purpose here, therefore letting go of all our old

responsibilities of doing it all. (Our one pure purpose is the gift and talent that is left when much all else falls away.)

In the higher realms, much of everything is really "hands off." We cannot take **responsibility**, for instance, for the experiences and growth of another. I can't tell you how many times I have seen well-intentioned people meddling in a soul growth experience of another or of the planet. It is rarely our **responsibility**, to save the planet through having a meditation for rain, for example. If we were to check in with the earth during each situation, the majority of time we would find that all was in divine and perfect order. Earth cleansings and purifications are vitally important for the process. The earth knows what she is doing, and can take care of herself. In regard to her residents, the majority of the time that we desire to meddle, individuals are having soul growth experiences, and "saving" them greatly interferes with their process. But most importantly, it pulls us away from our connection to Source, as we are "saving" from our ego or dis-connect selves. There are always exceptions to the above, as each situation is unique. This is why being connected is so vitally important. It tells us what is *really* going on.

Energy always knows what it is doing. There are "rules" and there is order in the cosmos...all relating to energy. Evolution, then, is simply following the "rules." Things get bad in order for a summoning to occur. A summoning creates a higher way, and so forth. It is not our **responsibility** to help and assist at every turn. If we do, we only block, complicate, and lengthen the process. We also interfere with the process of summoning. So if you have found yourself greatly backing off from becoming involved or taking **responsibility** for much, it is only because you are evolving into a higher level being.

The highest of the higher level non-physical beings *never* meddle...they wait to be asked, and even then, they sometimes do not answer as they do not wish to interfere with our individual process of finding out and growing on our own. A lower level non-physical being will answer all your questions and be there morning, noon, and night, therefore interfering with your own connection to Source by not allowing you to *be* Source yourself. Non-solicited visitation from a non-physical being is rarely good. There are always exceptions, of course, as there are times when we need to know something important. When I meet with the Star Beings, we have a community meeting area in a portal out in nature, as they do not believe in entering the sanctuary of my home. They are highly respectful. Others will come when I call, but only for specific purposes. In this way, I can strengthen my own connection to Source, as *I am* Source, as are you. So you see, at higher levels of existence, no one takes **responsibility** for another. It is simply not the way.

To reach the higher realms, we have to be free and clear. It is about being in the moment. It is about no attachments. It is about having that greater connection to Source because we are no longer connected to much else. There is a pattern and there is order here. It is an intentional process.

If you have chosen this page, you are being asked to let go of your old illusions of **responsibility**. Letting go of attachments is part of the process. And as you connect more strongly to Source, you will come to know that you need not do it all yourself.

REST

...

THE ASCENSION PROCESS can take a great toll on the body and the emotions. Like a continual roller coaster ride, this amazing and one-of-a-kind process creates sometimes traumatic and ground shaking experiences with ramifications like no other.

"I can't take any more!" you may exclaim at times. Or perhaps "What *else* can possibly happen?" The ascension process really puts us through the ringer. With so much energy moving at times, creating stress and the old familiar purging and releasing scenario, there are times when we need a break. We may think that we can stretch no further.

I can remember having extreme reactions during the on-set of my ascension experience several years ago. My body was so exhausted from all the internal restructuring going on, that I became exhausted even trying to have a phone conversation. The simple act of conversing and even *breathing*, totally wore me out. Through trial and error, I discovered that if I really rested, it greatly helped with the assimilation of these New and higher energies that were bombarding the planet. I needed all the body support I could get and thus needed to conserve my strength.

With a great amount of **rest**, most of the ascension symptoms I was experiencing were greatly diminished. Taking a 3D form and restructuring it into a higher vibrating and crystalline form is quite a process indeed.

In the old 3D reality we were conditioned that hard work was a great asset and was the real way to get anywhere. Not being very busy and not continually doing, doing, and doing was considered laziness and something very negative. Working hard for what we wanted, and pushing and striving were highly revered. In the higher realms this is not the case. Putting yourself first and really taking care of *you* is a much higher way of being. When we put ourselves first, the Universe gets the message and follows along. "Oh, so *this* is what we are doing!" the Universe responds.

Extreme self-care is vital for a more comfortable ascension process. If we take care of ourselves, the Universe will take care of us too. If you are able to give yourself permission to take a certain amount of designated time for you, you will find yourself in a wonderful space of receiving. This space is also the space of the higher realms. Self care and taking time to **rest** and smell the roses will place you in alignment with the higher realms and higher ways of being. And you do not have to be ill with the flu or some other manifestation to rationalize being in this space! Just tell yourself that Karen gave you permission!

In the higher realms, it is all about *being*. Being forced to **rest** through the rigors of the ascension process greatly assists in getting us used to this New and higher way. It is a natural by-product. *Doing* is a thing of the past. Slowing down and **resting** when needed along with *being* is surely the way to go. This is one reason why we can no longer do so much. We are not supposed to. We are literally being re-wired and trained for this New and higher way.

When we learn to take time for ourselves, the Universe will take care of the "rest." If we continue to try and do everything ourselves, we only get in the way and the Universe cannot do its job. As we are becoming more of Source energy ourselves through the ascension process, we are then learning to work in unity and partnership with Source and this involves learning to *slow down.* When we know when it is time to **rest** and are not concerned about resting often, we are then more primed for aligning with Source. We receive more messages. We connect more often. We see more clearly. We become much more of Source ourselves.

If you have chosen this page, you are ready for a **rest**. It can really help if you can find a way to rationalize that resting is a higher way of being. You are not responsible for everything. You are allowed to **rest** and to *be*. You are supposed to. The Universe truly wants to help and is just waiting for you to give it a chance to step in by getting out of the way and **resting** for awhile. You can actually get more accomplished by allowing yourself this time, as it will really place you in alignment with the higher realms. This is where you need to be. Have a wonderful and restful time!

SERVICE

...

WHEN WE EXPERIENCE pain and loss ourselves, we connect much more to a state of compassion. Experiencing the many losses that ascension can bring, makes us step back. It forces us to examine what our lives are *currently* about and what we *really* want our lives to *then* be about. Experiencing a significant loss enables us to get clear about what truly matters to us, as all else seems to now be insignificant.

It is then that we are inspired to become the humanitarian. Although we may have done humanitarian work and lived a life with **service** as a regular component in the past, the ascension process creates a need and desire for **service** at a whole New level and in an entirely different way.

Through ascension, we grow and expand through direct experience. It is very *real*. In this way, we are truly embodying New and higher states of being. We are walking our talk. We are *being* our talk. We have been there. We are now vibrating higher. In the past, we may have felt a desire to be of service, but it was not really the same. For the most part, it came from a different place. After we have had direct experience through the trials and tribulations that the ascension process brings, we are then embodying loss and suffering ourselves, as well as the corresponding contribution of compassion through **service**.

One of the outcomes and purposes of the ascension process involves evolving over a period of time into human angels. Eventually, we will surpass the current angels and non-physical beings ourselves, but before we do this, we will take on their roles. So then, we reach a point through the process of ascension where we are very called to do humanitarian work. Even though we may not have done this type of work for awhile, we are now ready to do it again, but in a very different way. As we are now *being* the light so much more, we have a lot to offer. And our level of compassion is at a New high and at a deeper and more real level.

After we reached critical mass on planet Earth in August of 2005, moved into the higher realms as a group in January of 2006, and completed our integration process in May of 2006, we were now ready to create a New and higher vibrating planet Earth. It was around this time that many losses were experienced in regard to our loved ones. Those close to us, whether they be in human or animal form, seemed to be leaving the earth plane in droves. They were taking with them all the lower vibrating aspects of our past. But having these experiences of loss, really made us step back and examine our lives. These loved ones knew exactly what they were doing at soul levels, as they knew that their departures would catapult us into a whole New space...a space of compassion and **service** and a space of being finally ready to create what we really wanted and knew we had to have...a higher vibrating reality.

So you see, there is always a perfect plan being played out. Everything is orchestrated at higher levels for the success and on-ward movement of our ascension plan. Becoming human angels of the earth, is part of the plan. As we have already had many challenging experiences ourselves, we are then ready to assist others on their journeys through our understanding and compassion. With impending natural disasters upon us, creating much loss for many, there is also a willingness and openness created for them to embrace and allow a New and higher way to now enter their lives and become their New reality.

If you have chosen this page, you are readying to begin your **service** work. Your passion and contribution may well be part of this work, as you begin to share your unique contribution for the creation of a New and higher vibrating world, with those who have experienced loss. With critical mass being reached, it activates within us a desire to capture the remaining parts of the world and bring them up in vibration. You may have a strong sense and knowing that lower vibrating realities will simply not be allowed. Simply allow this desire for **service** within you, to guide you to where you need and want to be...and watch your angel wings begin to expand and grow!

SIMPLICITY

...

ALL OF THE LETTING GO, loss, releasing, and endings created though the ascension process can ultimately leave us in a space of **simplicity**. There is such a beauty in **simplicity**. The joy of being there for a child's smile, watching a hawk fly across the sky, tending to a flower bed, watching your favorite Disney cartoon, sliding down the slide with your grandchild, or perhaps just observing an ant carrying a bite of food home.

Simplicity greatly frees us up to become a part of the moment. It frees us up to be much more present for what truly matters to us. As we become weary and apathetic through the ascension process, we cannot help but end up with a more simplistic life-style. With a busy, hectic life-style, we are really neither here nor there. And even though we may complain that ascension has taken so much from us, it has really left only what matters behind.

In **simplicity**, we have few responsibilities. We are so much more free, and we have all complained that we truly value our freedom! Within the freedom of **simplicity**, we can connect much more easily to Source. Our time is our own. We are removed from that busy and hectic world. In **simplicity**, we are able to see things we never had the time to notice before. Our lives move at a much slower pace. We can be present for others. We can be present for ourselves.

One of my favorite memories is sitting in an inner-tube, floating down the Russian River in the wine country of California, with my daughter, then eleven years old, and two of her friends. I do think I spent more time in those days with my daughter's friends than my own, as they were always so much more fun, had more innocence, and didn't question much. And we loved to play! That particular time, as we lived just down the street from the river, it just seemed a natural thing to do. And now I get to play with my grandchildren. We get into so much mischief...sloshing through the mud puddles, drawing, twirling around in the shopping carts at the store...oh, the **simplicity**!

Ascension brings back the **simplicity**. We don't have to take care of so many things. We have been removed from much of our prior responsibilities. We get to spend a good deal of time in our creativity. The child-like joy of our original and innocent inner child can re-emerge. And there are so many worlds within worlds that were unnoticed when we were in our busy, adult, and very serious lives. I can remember having my forehead down upon the earth out in nature one day on my friend's ranch in Colorado. Lo and behold, I discovered an entire civilization within the earth! It was truly amazing, and a sight to see. I would never have know that it was there if I hadn't been out just wandering around and enjoying myself, while my friend was off tending to "business!"

Thinking back on the creak of the ranch door when it opened, or the brilliant sunlight that flooded the living room when the door was left ajar...these are the fondest of memories. These are the precious moments. And these are the times that we can feel oh so joyful and blissful, and they do not involve material things or things that we feel we need for security. These times of **simplicity** are when spirit is ever present.

When I do not have a simple life, I feel very disconnected. Having no debt, being able to do pretty much whatever I want to whenever I want to, having the simplest of possessions, and having no real agenda, is the only way I feel comfortable these days. I would have a very difficult time having to be somewhere at a specified time…I'm just not used to it. If my life begins to get busy and complicated, I refuse to participate. **Simplicity** is much too valuable to me.

If you have chosen this page, you are being encouraged to remember that **simplicity** can bring you closer to Source. It can place you much more in the moment and allow things to arrive in a harmonious and synchronistic way of aligning very naturally through Source. Enjoy your **simplicity**…it's really what it's all about!

SUFFERING

...

ALTHOUGH **SUFFERING** MAY seem ungodly or perhaps even a lower vibrating experience, it actually has a very specific purpose. **Suffering** brings us much closer to Source and also creates compassion. When we are **suffering**, we are much more open and allowing, and when we are open, willing, and allowing, Source energy can then fill us to a much greater degree.

When we are **suffering**, we are much more "out of the way." But most importantly, we let go and are willing to allow something New and different to arrive for us. At times we can get desperate when we are **suffering**, and this is when we let go. Much else in our surrounding reality can seem inconsequential, and this is what creates the letting go and giving up. When we are **suffering**, we realize that we cannot solve whatever is ailing us, ourselves. These are the things that bring us back to Source. These are the things that get us out of the way. These are the things that cause us to surrender.

And when we have **suffered** ourselves, we develop great compassion for others. After we have gone through an experience of **suffering**, we then seem much more ready and in alignment to assist others, or perhaps become involved in some kind of humanitarian work.

When we **suffer**, we go deep. We feel deeply. We examine deeply. And we ask for help. When we ask for help and really mean it, we usually receive it. But we have to get out of the way first and let go of our ego or in-charge self. This is all a vital part of the ascension process. **Suffering** is another way that we connect more deeply and strongly to Source. After we have connected through **suffering**, we can then remember what this connection feels like and utilize it again, only in a non-suffering situation. We remember that Source was very present and we can then summon Source again to help others.

Viewing **suffering** from the higher realms, it looks very different. In the higher realms, it is known that life comes and goes and that energy infuses here and then it infuses there. When looking back at a **suffering** experience after one has left their physical body, one does not feel that this experience was any big deal. This is the way it is. It is known that this is a part of being in the physical world. Emotions are very valued, as they are one of the things that being in form is all about. **Suffering** is simply another experience and no big deal. But we sure think it is when we are the ones who are suffering!

Suffering and compassion are basically partners. And compassion is a very high vibrating state of emotion. Being that **suffering** creates a vibrational change in a person and also creates an opening to Source, as well as at times a summoning for the New, we can then see that watching **suffering** in another is not something we need to meddle in or become involved in alleviating. This is not always a set rule, of course. The non-physical beings watch us **suffer** continually and never meddle. And this is why. They are simply honoring our process. And as we are becoming the human angels of the earth, we will need to adopt this higher way of being as well. I can tell you from experience, it's not easy...but it is part of our evolutionary process. Therefore, it is important that we understand and value **suffering** for what it is and what it produces.

If you have chosen this page, you are being asked to understand the higher role of **suffering**. When you are able to embrace the process that **suffering** creates, you will be well on your way to becoming a higher vibrating human.

THE EARTH

...

STRANGE AS IT MAY seem, we ascend through the **earth**. In our 3D minds, we may have envisioned ourselves being lifted up into the cosmos, or perhaps have always felt that Heaven was in the clouds, but in all actuality, it is really about Mother **Earth** and Father Sky. Yes, there are most certainly higher vibrating energies arriving from above, but also remember that there are also New energetic portals opening within the **earth** as well.

The **earth** contains many hidden secrets. Eons ago, many of us knew what would be coming in regard to a darker and denser scenario on the planet **earth**. And eons ago, these many were also the original creators of the **earth** as well. With this great love for the **earth** and this higher knowledge of the secrets of the **earth** in tow, these souls buried these higher vibrating secrets in order to keep them safe.

Then along came ascension. The ascension process involved raising the vibration of the **earth**, as well as every living thing upon her, including her inhabitants. It was time for the original blueprint of the **earth** to be restored. When the vibration began to rise through the ascension process, it signaled a time of opening on the **earth**. First began the opening of what had been concealed and hidden during the time of Lemuria. The area that opened first, then, was around the Hawaiian Islands and into Southern California. As the vibration of the **earth** continued to rise exponentially, other areas began to open as well...the UK, Australia, and Africa, to name a few.

In this way, the **earth** is then carrying a higher vibration herself. And in the very near future, we will be remembering many of her secrets. The **earth** is here to provide our every need. All that we could ever want is contained on and within the **earth**. She is the blue jewel, the keeper of all, and the doorway to other dimensions. As consciousness can only evolve through form, she is the form, as are we.

Our current society and ways of living have totally forgotten about where they are residing...on the **earth** herself. Outer technology does much for us that we no longer remember how to do ourselves. We have forgotten how to tell time by looking at the sun. We have lost our ability to intuitively know what the weather patterns will be. We spend very little time on the **earth** herself, as we are usually inside dwellings or in cars. We have become disconnected from the **earth**. We have forgotten how important it is to live in harmony with her ways...even though we reside on her!

The **earth** has the higher knowledge and wisdom of higher realms reality. The ancients knew this, and utilized the **earth** and the celestial bodies in their everyday lives. They knew when to plant, what planets were influencing them and when, and also knew what was to come. We are very much a part of the **earth**. We are made up of the same elements and can even consider ourselves a microcosm.

With the **earth** being such a higher vibrating entity, we could greatly benefit if we stayed continually connected to her. Studies have shown that just lying on her daily, immensely improves one's health, and even heals, as well as supporting a continual state of peace and calmness. If I do not have a daily connection with the earth, I get very wiggy and off-balance. Telling most of everyone, no matter what their spiritual orientation, that "The earth is my church," always brings a nod of agreement.

The **earth** has much to tell us now. She is ready to reveal her long hidden secrets. If you have chosen this card, know that your ascension process can be greatly supported through re-connecting with the **earth**. This powerful, sometimes overlooked, and highly vibrating Source is there for us to utilize right now. The **earth** is our doorway to ascension. It is *through* her, that we can continue to be in alignment with the higher realms. By choosing this page, you are being encouraged to connect to the **earth**. Try and turn off your TV, computer and phones. Spend more time with your feet directly upon her, eat organic, go camping or hiking, work in your garden, take a daily walk in nature, become involved with sustainability, or simply partake in anything made from the **earth**.

TRUST

...

"**TRUST, TRUST**, AND **trust** some more." This could easily be one of the most pivotal mantras of the ascension process. Going through this many times confusing process can create feelings of bewilderment and perhaps leave one wondering if everything and anything is in divine right order at all.

As the ascension process slowly but surely creates a higher level and higher vibrating human, when we reach these New and higher ways of being, they are not always how we expected them to be. And with so much leaving our lives along with so much change occurring, we may wonder what in the world is going on.

Even though we may not consciously know at the time why and what our lives are evolving into, simply **trusting** in the process can bring us great comfort and relief. At lower levels things may not make sense. But at the higher dimensional levels they always make perfect sense. Although the phrase "All is always in divine right order," may at times sound trite and repetitive, and get old as well, when we are able to see through personal experience that this process is in total perfection, that old, trite phrase begins to make some sense.

Over and over again, as I have viewed things from a higher dimensional level, the perfection is always evident. Things are always working like a perfectly oiled machine. And even though it may appear otherwise, these strange and confusing experiences are here to support us in every way.

For instance, one typical higher level scenario involves the separation of partners. So many times I have seen individuals go through what they interpret as an "error" or a painful experience of being left behind or "dumped" by their romantic partner. This painful experience usually places them in the victim posture. What is almost always occurring is an immense expression of love at higher soul levels. One partner knows that the other is ready to experience more of their higher purpose, or ready to expand and grow, and hence, will then leave the other in order to give him/her this very important opportunity.

In this same arena, another scenario can also express itself. Partners separate because the vibration of the planet has reached a certain level. Before we were born, we agreed to fulfill certain roles and purposes. Each of us has several soul partners and there are many in our soul groups. We came to serve as companions and supporters for each other...not necessarily as romantic partners. When the planet reaches certain frequencies, we are then activated according to our pre-birth plans. In this regard, we separate from those we have been with during certain phases of the ascension process. We need to now fulfill New and different roles, and therefore, need to go in different directions. At lower levels this may manifest as a sudden "not able to get along" experience and reality. But the truth of the matter is that at the higher levels, we need to separate and will then create an impetus at lower levels. If we are not fully conscious at higher soul levels, scenarios will then occur that inevitably get us where we need and have chosen to be.

There is always great and expansive love at higher soul levels. This is also very evident in regard to the love shown us by our non-physical "guides" or those non-physical beings that have chosen to watch over us during this process. We are never abandoned here. We are only left alone so that we can grow and expand through experience. Losing jobs, loved ones, money, or our health are all part of the process designed to get us where we need to be. Things are always being navigated at higher dimensional levels.

If you have chosen this page, you are being reminded that all is in divine and perfect order. You are being asked to **trust**, even though you may not be consciously aware of the reasons for your current experience. As you evolve through the ascension process, and rise to higher levels enabling you to "see" beyond the veil, you will in time come to know and understand what this experience was all about.

WILLINGNESS

...

WILLINGNESS IS DIFFERENT from acceptance and allowing. It is not as passive or receptive. By being **willing**, we are telling the Universe that we are very ready. It is much more purposeful and intentional. We are much more in charge.

I had a friend a few years ago, who at age 65, was really going through her ascension paces. It's a wonder she didn't pass away with all the health situations she was experiencing. She explained to me that she believed that by being **willing**, she created a summoning for a more rapid process of spiritual growth. She believed that she had summoned this process **willingly**, as she was very dedicated to her spiritual growth.

While *accepting* and *allowing* the ascension process to occur, creates a much more relaxed physical vessel for all the New and higher vibrating energies to come through, **willingness** can actually begin the process, or be the precursor for the next stage to arrive for us. By being **willing** to experience a New energy or way of being, these occurrences, then, will arrive much more frequently. It is almost as if we are agreeing to be a guinea pig for the higher ways, in order to pave the way for others to follow.

Willingness says, "I am ready to move forward with complete certainly." **Willingness** says, "Let's roll." **Willingness** lets *us* decide when we are ready for the next step. Loss is more of a situation that seems out of our control...as seem most of the ascension symptoms and experiences. The ascension process seems to have a mind of its' own...never mind what we want or believe! Even though this is not the case, being **willing** can help us to feel more at the helm.

When we are **willing**, we place ourselves into a space where we are basically saying that we *remember*. We remember why we are here during this particular time on Earth. We remember that we agreed to participate in this amazing and one-of-a-kind experience of raising our vibrations and the vibrations of the planet through physical form. We remember that we agreed that we would start over, with a very New beginning, and in order to do that we agreed to transmute any darker and lower vibrating energies. By being **willing**, we are stepping more fully into the shoes of our soul plan. We are more in alignment with it. We are then working together with our souls as a team. We are not acting like victims who are having a non-voluntary experience. We volunteered...remember?

By being **willing**, we can take over our ascension process, instead of letting it take over us. If you have chosen this page, you are being reminded that you are actually at the helm, even though you may not feel this is the case. **Willingness** will bring on more of an intentional ascension experience. It tells the Universe that we are ready for the next step, even though we do not know what it will be. It tells the Universe that we trust in the process that is unfolding before us. It is more than getting out of the way and allowing Source to do what it needs to do. It puts us in a better partnership as co-creators with Source and reminds us that our souls know exactly what they are doing.

YOUR ASCENSION GUIDE

...

AS WE NAVIGATE through this confusing and many times challenging process of ascension, we may feel very alone and vulnerable. It can seem as though we have been dropped here on Earth with no support to handle all that is happening to us. Believe it or not, this is not the case.

Each and every one of us has a beautiful **ascension guide** who monitors our progress at each and every turn. This process of ascension was created by us at soul levels. We decided to raise the consciousness (or vibration) of Earth as a group, through ourselves, in order to begin again. We have to go through this process ourselves by experiencing it firsthand. This can create moments of disconnect, chaos, fear, and near everything else. So for the most part, we certainly do not feel at the helm ourselves.

I first became aware of **ascension guides** when I was reading the energy of a friend going through the process. Lo and behold, there standing right next to her was a big, beautiful non-physical being who was practically "guarding" her as she went through her process. This being was making sure that things did not get out of hand and go too far. He (it) was making sure that she was benefiting and growing through her process as it had been planned, instead of having the process weaken or destroy her. **Ascension guides** are here to make sure that nothing goes too far in regard to our "stretching."

The next encounter I had with an **ascension guide** was when I connected with my own. I was having a really rough time and basically coming unglued. In popped this huge non-physical being who proceeded to tell me that it was my attitude that was making everything far worse than it needed to be. From that day forward, I knew that someone was indeed *there* for me, and what a wonderful feeling it was.

Any non-physical beings that we are especially connected to, rarely interfere with our process (if they are highly vibrating beings). And this is especially true for **ascension guides**. Although they need to be especially "hands off," they come from a deep place of love and caring for us. And know too, that we are going through this process for them as well. They freely admit this and are therefore very grateful and highly respectful of who we are and what we are doing. We are ascending for all of the cosmos. Even though they know more than we consciously do right now, we will eventually surpass them.

It is a sure fact that we are the stars of the show. All the attention and the lights are on us, as we progress through this process of ascension. There is so much help and support on board, even though we may not be able to see or sense it at times. It is because we are on the front-lines. We are in the thick of it. So at times, we cannot see the forest for the trees.

All of this said, here's a little secret. Our **ascension guides** are really only higher vibrating aspects of ourselves. When I finally sat down and really read the energy of my ascension guide, I truly remembered who I was. I WAS THIS GREAT, ANCIENT, AND MAGNIFICENT BEING. What an eye-opener this was. And as I connected the dots, I could clearly see that this being had been there for me all along. He (it) had been at the foot of my bed in the year 2000, telling me that something that would change me forever was about to occur. He had been at my hospital bedside after I had shattered my leg. He had been there when I was whining to no end during my ascension process, and now he is here as a true and good friend who continues to connect me to the higher realms through himself. These beings bring in the higher energies. We are able to connect much higher when we begin vibrating much higher. It is then that we are with them on a much more regular basis. As we begin vibrating higher and higher, we will then connect with much higher guides, but we will really be only connecting with much higher aspects of ourselves.

If you find yourself having a difficult time, know that you may call on your **ascension guide**. If you are not particularly psychic, just ask for a sign. Ask your guide to show you that he (it) is there. Ask your guide to deliver to you in a form that you can easily receive, what you currently need to know to assist you on your journey. Whether it be a passage in a book, a phrase from a conversation from a friend, or perhaps something on TV, you can ask that a message be given to you.

Asking for a sign is a good way to validate something if you don't have a lot of psychic ability, or even if you do and are just very stressed and cannot connect very well right then. One time, right before my ascension process really began, I needed a job. I was getting downloads of information that fit in with not "working" anymore, but I wasn't quite there yet. I got hired as the director for the United Way. I didn't really want to do that kind of thing anymore...I had done it forever. So I quit after one day. Boy, I certainly sound like a flake, but I wanted to stay in alignment! After this, I didn't trust my judgment much. None-the-less, I gave things some thought, and I decided that I would really love to be a grant writer...it fit in well with a lot about me. But I was afraid of going down the wrong road once again, so I asked for a sign. While in the dusty back rooms of the local newspaper office one day, looking through their archives, as I had remembered an ad for a grant writer weeks earlier, I got my sign. I was unable to locate the ad. As I put up the last huge bound archive book, there was nothing left on the dusty table below it but an old, outdated newspaper page. On it was an ad for a department store, and in absolutely huge letters was the word GRANTS. So I got my sign, the flood gates flew open with many synchronicities, and I became a trained grant writer within weeks.

But here's another little secret. There is really no one deciding our path for us or letting us know what we should or shouldn't be doing. I received the grant writing confirmation because I created it myself. I was much more in alignment with it than anything else. We're the ones that make a path right...we're the ones that are the powerful creators. When we ask for a sign, just like our **ascension guides,** it is really us giving the sign. We just don't trust our own judgment yet and like to place the power outside of ourselves because we think something out there knows more than we do. We are far greater creators than we believe. Handing our power over to something else, gets us out of the way, which is a perfect energetic alignment for creating!

If you have chosen this page, know that you are not alone. We each have a loving and protective **ascension guide** at our side who is monitoring our progress at each and every turn. Even though these amazing and caring beings are really aspects of ourselves, they still exist in the forms that we picture them in. They are *us* in our future state, and therefore love and care about us like no one else. Thank goodness for **ascension guides**!

About The Author

Karen Bishop is the creator of *What's Up On Planet Earth?*, a website devoted to the ascension process and life in the higher realms. Recognized as an authority on ascension, Karen has reached thousands of readers worldwide through her weekly energy alerts about human and planetary evolution, along with the latest information about ascension symptoms and our current planetary status, since 2002.

A life-long clairvoyant, multidimensional traveler and communicator, she has also undergone the challenges of the ascension process . Inspired to use her gifts and talents to reach others going through this amazing on-going evolutionary experience, she continues to give the latest information of our ascension process and life in the higher realms through her mini book series and website.

With an educational background in psychology, counseling and law, Karen has served as a facilitator, counselor and teacher, working with county agencies, non-profit agencies, Native American tribes, public school systems and various individuals.

Currently residing in the mountains of Northeastern Arizona, she follows her joy and passion through writing, sewing fabric art for home interiors (now as a hobby), painting, weaving, enjoying her animals and time in nature, and communicating with and experiencing the higher realms. She is currently working on her mini book series *Life In The Higher Realms*.

For more information about Karen and her latest messages and writings about the ascension process and life in the higher realms, please visit her website at: *www.whatsuponplanetearth.com*. You may contact Karen through her website.

Printed in the United States
67334LVS00002B/2